REMARKABLE
ROAD
TRIPS

First published in the United Kingdom in 2019 by
Pavilion Books,
43 Great Ormond Street,
London WC1N 3HZ

Produced by Salamander Editorial
Part of the Remarkable series which includes
Remarkable Cricket Grounds, *Remarkable Golf Courses*,
Remarkable Racecourses and *Remarkable Village
Cricket Grounds*.

ISBN 978-1-911641-01-8

A CIP catalogue record for this book is available from
the British Library.

10 9 8 7 6 5 4 3 2 1

Reproduction by Rival UK

Printed and bound by 1010 Printing International

Author's Acknowledgements
My thanks to Simon Dures, Fiona Scott-Barrett and
Jonathan Trew for additional research.

Cover photo: Driving into the sunset in Phattalung,
Thailand.
Contents page: The Wild Atlantic Way at Achill Island in
County Mayo, Ireland.

REMARKABLE ROAD TRIPS

— COLIN SALTER —

EDITOR
FRANK HOPKINSON

PAVILION

Contents

Introduction

Road trips have several advantages over other forms of travel. You see far more of the land through which you drive, instead of flying far above it. You are in control of your route and can stop at will, instead of being confined to the halts along a railway line for example. And you can go a lot further than you can by bicycle or on foot, although some of our routes are as exhilarating to walk or pedal as they are to drive.

For many intrepid travellers, it's all about the journey, not about the destination at all. If that's you, then I suggest you just start at the beginning of this book and work your way through. Every one of the trips takes you through a different landscape, from the vineyards of Alsace to the icefields of Canada via the salt flats of Bolivia and the seventy hairpin bends of the Stelvio Pass.

There are routes in Europe, Asia, Australasia, North and South America, along coasts, across deserts and through mountains. We take you around busy capital cities and to remote villages. The shortest trip in this book is just 2.7 miles (4.3 km) long, the longest over 1,600 miles (2,500 km). For the avoidance of confusion we've listed distances in the local unit of measurement – so trips in the United Kingdom and the United States are given in miles, but elsewhere we measure in kilometres. Although when it comes to mountains that you won't be driving directly up, just standing back and admiring, we have used both metres and feet.

LEFT: The scenic road through the Grand Staircase-Escalante National Monument in Utah, USA.

Mountains feature heavily in our selection, with their dramatic views and often perilous ascents. The Transfăgărășan Road is a classic European pass route taking you over the Carpathian Mountains in Romania. The North Yungas Road in Bolivia on the other hand clings to the side of sheer cliffs, sometimes even running behind waterfalls. Officially designated the Most Dangerous Road in the World and known as the Road of Death, many sections of it are lined with memorials to those who misjudged one corner too many.

Coastal routes can be just as vertiginous, and just as visually rewarding. The Amalfi coast road in Italy combines twisting clifftop roadways with beautiful, precariously perched hillside villages and sparkling sea views. Scotland's recently devised North Coast 500 trail hugs the most northerly shores of mainland Britain, formed from some of the most spectacular and ancient geology in Europe. Our shortest route, the Passage du Gois, is underwater for eighteen hours a day. Time your visit carefully.

Some road trips are also journeys through time. Recent history oozes from every kilometre of the Ho Chi Minh Road in Vietnam. Along Germany's Romantische Strasse the castles and walled towns tell the countryside's medieval story, before modern Germany existed. In France the Grande Route des Alpes is lined with ancient fortresses guarding passes against its neighbour Italy. Canada's Cabot Trail and the White Mountain Ring in the US both take you in the footsteps of their countries' earliest settlers.

ABOVE LEFT: Our routes take you past some classic architecture, in this instance the mellow Cotswold stone houses of Stanton, part of the Cotswold Market Towns tour.

LEFT: Go out of season and many of the roads will be tricky, some impassable. This is Canada's Icefield Parkway in Banff.

RIGHT: Take some UV protection on the highly reflective salt flat of Salar de Uyuni. The air is thin at the dizzying height of 3,656 metres (11,995 ft) above sea level.

We have not forgotten lovers of the city environment. Within these pages you'll find routes through London and Paris, and another concentrating on the Art Deco architectural heritage of Miami. But many routes leave the man-made world behind in favour of an extended immersion in nature. The endless kilometres of Canada's Dempster Highway cross one of the world's last wildernesses, a remarkably varied landscape of mountains, plateaux and tumbling rivers in which you will cross the Arctic Circle and pass only two fuel stops. The Hana Highway in Hawaii passes through an extraordinary diversity of forest life, both leafed and feathered. Monument Valley in Utah has a unique geology. It is wonderful just to drive through such scenery. But the best moments of any road trip are the moments when you stop driving – when you pull over and get out of the car to stretch your legs and just Be There. Breathe the air. Touch the soil. Listen to the birds. Speak to the people. Whether you're a seasoned traveller or an armchair motorist, these road trips will transport you to other worlds. But a journey doesn't only move you geographically. Travel is mind-expanding. Turn these pages and open your mind to new places and people on and off the beaten track. Enjoy the drive.

Colin Salter
2019

RIGHT: The Kylesku Bridge just north of Unapool, part of the increasingly popular North Coast 500, in Scotland.

BELOW: Many of these routes have been described as 'trips of a lifetime'. The Road of Death in Bolivia can certainly shorten that lifetime.

Amalfi Coast Road

Italy

Length: 86 km, 54 miles
Start: Salerno
Finish: Sorrento
Highlights: Minori, Ravello, Positano, the Sirenuses, Sorrento

The Amalfi Coast Road traverses an area described by UNESCO as a classic Mediterranean landscape that offers outstanding scenery and displays diverse cultural and historical influences. It's also great fun to drive.

Many sections are 'corniche' (running alongside a cliff or mountain) and present breathtaking views of the turquoise waters of the Tyrrhenian Sea below. Designated viewing points along the roads allow drivers to stop and admire the vista, but at busy times of the year these fill up fast. It is not uncommon for sightseers to pull over anywhere on the side of the road, reducing what is already a narrow road to a hazardous width.

The Amalfi Coast Road runs along the southern fringe of the mountainous Sorrento Peninsula, which overlooks the Gulf of Naples to the north, and the Gulf of Salerno to the south. The best place to join the road, the SS 163, is at the village of Vietri sul Mare, 6 km southwest of the port of Salerno. From here the road leads west for 37 km, twisting and winding through

RIGHT: The village of Atrani just east of Amalfi. The road sweeps round the Collegiate Church of St Mary Magdelene.

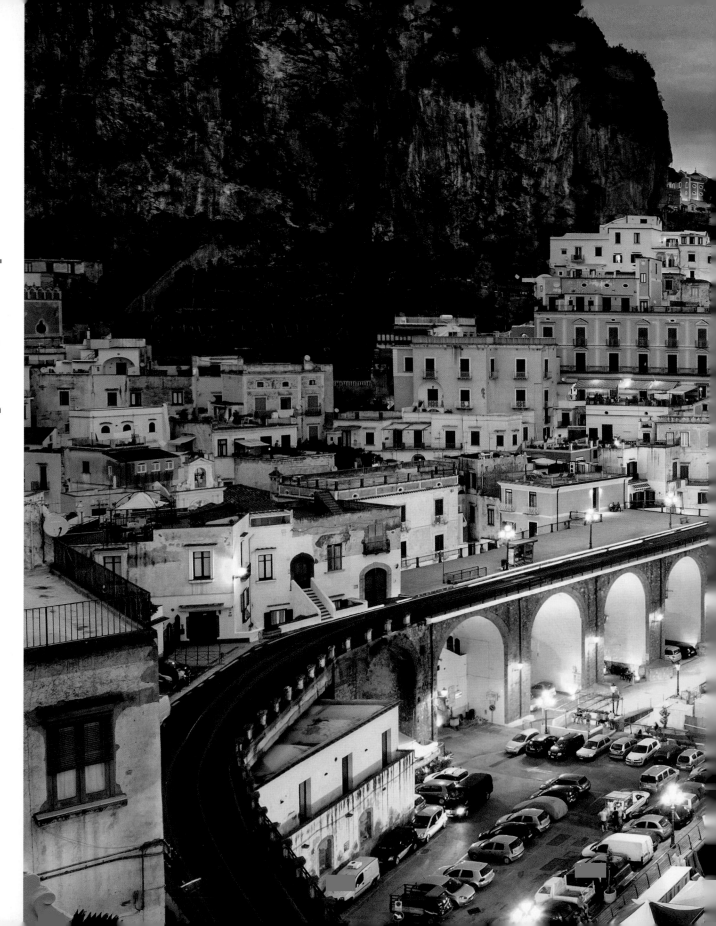

spectacular landscapes of cliffs, luxuriant gardens, terraced vineyards and lemon groves as well as picturesque villages that cling to the mountainside.

From the village of Minori, where those interested in archaeology can visit the ruins of a first-century Roman villa, the road turns to the south-west. About 2.5 km along this stretch, and shortly before the village of Atrani, the Hotel Villa San Michele lies to the left of the road. Immediately after that, the road forks. The right

fork is the SS 373, which leads up through a series of hairpin bends to the town of Ravello. This delightful small town has been associated with writers since the 14th-century Italian author Boccaccio set his famous work *The Decameron* in Ravello's Villa Rufolo, which was built in 1272. More recent writers who have lived or spent time in Ravello include Virginia Woolf, Andre Gide, Tennessee Williams and Gore Vidal. The composer Richard Wagner also lived in Ravello for a while, and a music festival takes place in the town every summer to honour him. The town

also boasts a cathedral dating from the 11th century, a number of smaller churches, and jaw-dropping views of the sea below.

Keeping to the left fork past the Hotel Villa San Michele, the SS 163 continues on to Amalfi, once the capital of the Duchy of Amalfi, one of Italy's four great maritime republics. Nowadays, the town is a popular resort and is known for the production of limoncello, a lemon liqueur and of handmade paper. Tourists can visit the 11th-century cathedral or the Museum of Handmade

Paper, or just relax in a café and soak up the atmosphere of this pretty pastel-painted town overlooking the sea.

Continuing west from Amalfi, roughly the halfway point of this trip, the corniche road becomes even more dramatic, passing over stone viaducts and through tunnels carved into the mountainside. Beside the oncoming lane there are dizzying drops to the sea, protected only by a railing or low stone wall. The next place of interest is the colourful small town of Positano, which climbs from sea level steeply up the mountainside and boasts excellent views of the whole coastline. Positano has featured in several films, and was for a while the home of the Italian film director Franco Zeffirelli.

After Positano, the scenery is rockier and more rugged and the area is less populated. The road hugs the coast for another 9 km, continuing in a series of bends, then turns inland opposite the small archipelago known as the Sirenuses. These

islands are so called because they were said to be home to mythological sirens – creatures that were half-bird, half-woman whose beautiful singing and music lured sailors to their death.

From this point, the road heads across the Sorrentine peninsula in a north-westerly direction, and the sea is no longer visible. In the municipality of Piano di Sorrento, the SS 163 merges into the SS 143, which leads northwest and descends into the resort of Sorrento on the northern coast of the peninsula.

The Amalfi Coast Road drive is widely acknowledged to be one of the most scenic drives in Europe, but it is not a road trip for the timid or inexperienced driver. The road is narrow and the traffic is frequently dense, especially in high season when there are tour buses on the road. The dramatic views can easily distract attention from the road and this adds to the danger. For confident and experienced drivers, however, it offers a thrilling ride.

OPPOSITE: The village of Minori is about 3.5 kilometres east of Amalfi and just west of Maiori.

BELOW LEFT: A typical Amalfi Coast vista. If you wanted to do 'the full Italian' you should travel the SS 163 by scooter.

BELOW: A panoramic view of journey's end, Sorrento. There's still time to take in Pompeii; it's only 26 kilometres away.

BOTTOM: Like retsina in Greece, limoncello tastes best when drunk in Amalfi.

The Atlantic Road

Norway

Length: 8 km, 5 miles
Start: Vevang
Finish: Kårvåg
Highlights: Storseisundet Bridge, Askevågen viewpoint

At its most extreme, the road's bridges dip and soar over the waves of the rugged Hustadvika coastline in the north-west of the country. If a storm is raging, the dividing line between land and sea can be blurred.

The Atlanterhausveien is an 8.4-km rollercoaster that links Averøy with the mainland. Connecting the villages of Kårvåg on Averøy and Vevang in Eida, the road hops and skips over a series of islands and skerries linked by causeways and seven bridges. It is part of a longer National Tourist Route which stretches between Bud and Kristiansund.

Opened in 1989, the road has been referred to as Norway's Engineering Feat of the Century, mainly due to its truly remarkable bridges. At

260 metres (755 ft) long and with a height of 23 metres (75 ft), the biggest is the cantilevered Storseisundet Bridge. From certain angles, the humpback shape of the bridge makes it look as though the road comes to an abrupt stop over the water. It's the bridge with the twist.

As well as restaurants, accommodation, diving shops and fishing charters, the islands have four resting places and lookout points which make the most of the Atlantic Road's location on the ocean's edge. The views change considerably depending on the season. The high latitude means that during the summer you might enjoy a balmy 10pm sunset over a mirror-like sea. If you are lucky, you could spot seals or even a sea eagle dropping by for supper. Drive the route on a darkening January afternoon and you might find yourself in the teeth of a gale which is buffeting the car and whipping ocean spray over the road.

If the weather is savage then the brave, or foolhardy, can step outside the car and feel the forces of nature from the Askevågen viewpoint. Built from artfully rusted steel and green glass walls, the open platform juts out over the water. Also known as 'The Road in the Ocean', the sinuous route has starred in many a car advert and motoring magazine. Watching the adverts may give a sense of the thrills it offers, but driving it – especially in wild weather – is a far more visceral experience.

LEFT: The Atlanterhausveien is good for both driving and fishing. There are fishing walkways along the route.

RIGHT: Unlike many of the routes; when the weather gets really bad on the Atlantic Road, the drive becomes more interesting.

Bay of Islands

North Island, New Zealand

Length: 439 km, 273 miles
Start: Auckland
Finish: Cape Reinga
Highlights: Whangarei Falls, Kawakawa public toilets, Paihia, Bay of Islands, Russell, Haruru Falls, Mangonui, Ninety Mile Beach, Cape Reinga

New Zealand's South Island gets all the attention from lovers of dramatic scenery, but Northland, the northernmost finger of North Island, has a quiet charm and drama of its own.

A drive through the Bay of Islands takes you to the country's earliest European roots and further back into the pre-European world of the Maoris. This is a journey of beginnings and endings. Auckland, at the south end of Northland, is

New Zealand's largest city, with a full third of the country's population. It is a magnet for the migrating populations of the Pacific rim and holds the largest single Polynesian population anywhere in the world. Only a little over half the city's inhabitants think of themselves as being of European origin, and the result is a culturally vibrant place.

A drive north from Auckland takes you to places where Maori and European traditions have met, places of sometimes sacred memory to one or other. Towns like Forrest Hill and Redhill, Redvale and Silverdale, soon give way to names from a different language like Puhoi, famous for its cheese and ice cream, and Matakana which has a wonderful Saturday farmers' market. Matakana,

OPPOSITE: An aerial view of the Bay of Islands shows exactly why it got the name.

BELOW LEFT: Kayaking at Haruru Falls, 3 kilometres inland from Paihia, New Zealand's first river port.

BELOW: Foodie heaven at the Saturday market in Matakana.

BOTTOM: Elegant structures abound in Whangarei, the northernmost city in New Zealand.

just off Route 1, is worth a detour if only to see its architecturally remarkable public toilets.

The biggest city north of Auckland is Whangarei, a thriving port blessed with a fine natural harbour protected by a narrow entrance between Whangarei Heads and Marsden Point. Here Captain Cook caught fish in 1769 and named the harbour Bream Bay. A classic curtain waterfall, Whangarei Falls to the north of the city, drops 26 metres (85 ft) from an ancient lava flow into a large swimming hole below.

Unusually, this is a road trip with not one but two must-see public conveniences. At Kawakawa there is another, known as the Bottle House because of the flattened bottles used as window glass. It was designed two years before his death by the eclectic Austrian architect Friedensreich Hundertwasser who made this area his home in the 1970s. He is buried in Rotarua south of Auckland. Construction began in 2018 on the Hundertwasser Art Gallery in Whangarei.

TOP LEFT: The wharf and ferry terminal at Russell. The fledgling settlement there was once mooted as the potential capital of New Zealand.

LEFT: The Strand at Russell.

BELOW: A ferry between Opua and Okiato takes cars a short distance across the Waikare Inlet.

Kawakawa is also home to the Bay of Islands Vintage Railway which runs down the middle of the main street past the Hundertwasser toilets.

The Northland journey here leaves Route 1 for Route 12 and heads down to Paihia, an ideal base from which to explore the Bay of Islands on one of the many cruises by sailing ship or jet boat. There are 144 islands in the bay, which was named (rather unimaginatively) by Captain Cook in 1769.

Later that century it was the first area of New Zealand to be colonized by Europeans. At Waitangi, just north of Paihia, a treaty was signed in 1840 between the British authorities and the Maori leaders of the day, guaranteeing protection and continued ownership of their lands. Differences in the Maori and English versions of the text gave rise to the New Zealand Wars between the two parties.

The treaty is seen as the start of the modern state of New Zealand and debates about it continue to shape the relationship between European New Zealanders and Maoris. Nowadays you can visit the Treaty Grounds, see the world's largest Maori war canoe and in a decorated wooden meeting house join with Maoris for a traditional welcome greeting or pōwhiri.

From Paihia there are regular ferries across the bay to Russell, a mainland town which is otherwise only accessible by a tortuous and very exposed coastal road (43 km or 2.3 km by boat). Russell is an attractive jumble of cafes and souvenir shops with the oldest pub and church in New Zealand (two different buildings). Inland from Paihia the Haruru Falls make a beautiful and deafening horseshoe – the name means 'big noise'.

Many return to Auckland after seeing the Bay of Islands; it's a popular day trip. But to come

BELOW: The Matakana rest rooms were designed by Steffan de Haan, a first-year student at Auckland University. Their shape reflects the importance of boat building in the area.

BOTTOM LEFT AND RIGHT: Two views of the famous Friedensreich Hundertwasser toilets in Kawakawa. The Austrian artist wanted to make it a special place, 'because you meditate in a toilet, like a church. The similarity is not so far fetched.'

all this way and not carry on to the northern tip of the island, where the land runs out and the Pacific Ocean meets the Tasman Sea, would be a wasted opportunity. Following the east coast of Northland the road passes several harbour towns. Mangonui is one of the prettiest, lined with old colonial houses and stores, home of New Zealand's best and possibly most expensive fish and chips.

You start to get a sense here of time and the landscape running out, of being at the end of things. The land flattens; there are fewer houses. At Houhara, there's little more than a café and New Zealand's most northerly bar. These last 65 km of New Zealand are no more than 10 km wide, and the whole of the west coast is one long expanse of sand. Ninety Mile Beach, as it is called – in fact only 55 miles (89 km) in length – is a designated highway, an exhilarating drive if you have the right vehicle. Most hire cars are not insured for it, and you don't have to take to the sands. There is still a tarmac road down the spine of this long pastoral goodbye to New Zealand.

It ends at Cape Reinga, from whose lighthouse on a calm day you can actually see the different colours of the Tasman Sea and the Pacific Ocean collide. On stormy days the collision can be quite spectacular. Anyone can feel the magic of the place, and it is a sacred Maori site. From an 800-year-old tree growing out of the cliff here, the souls of the dead fly out and into the ocean towards Hawaiki, the legendary homeland of all Polynesians. They have reached the end of one journey and the start of another, as you have: it's time to head back to Auckland.

TOP LEFT: The highly acclaimed Mangonui Fish Shop on the front at Mangonui Village.

LEFT: The lighthouse at Cape Reinga was the last manual lighthouse to be built in New Zealand (1941).

RIGHT: The rocky coastline at Cape Reinga.

The Black Forest High Panoramic Road

Germany

Length: 65 km, 41 miles
Start: Baden-Baden
Finish: Freudenstadt
Highlights: Geroldsau waterfall, Bühlerhöhe, Mehliskopf, Mummelsee, Allerheiligen monastery, Lotharpfad tower

The lofty Schwarzwaldhochstrasse (Black Forest High Road) is the oldest of several panoramic routes through the mountainous south-western corner of Germany. First devised in 1930, it was completed in its current form in 1952. Expect forests, lakes, beer – and of course, gateau.

Southern Germany was an early pioneer of scenic tourism and of dedicated routes through its natural splendour. The Weinstrasse (Wine Road) was established in 1935 and the Romantische Strasse (Romantic Road) in the 1950s. They evoked the spirit of the Grand European Tours undertaken by Britain's wealthier classes in the 18th and 19th centuries, but on a more manageable, middle-class scale.

Even with the motor vehicles and road surfaces of the 1930s, the Schwarzwaldhochstrasse could be completed comfortably over a weekend. In practice the opportunity for a series of exhilarating mountain walks persuaded many to take a week over it, providing valuable trade for a string of luxury alpine hotels along the way. The Black Forest has always been a popular hiking area.

Nowadays its route from Baden-Baden to Freudenstadt makes for a very leisurely day out. In the winter it also provides fast access to some great ski resorts. After the initial ascent from Baden-Baden the whole route remains between 800 and 1,000 metres (2,620–3,280 ft) above sea level. Baden-Baden is an ancient spa

town, whose waters were used by the Romans as a treatment for arthritis. It was the Romans who gave the Black Forest its name; its trees were denser and taller than anything they had seen in Italy. Modern Germans still visit Baden-Baden (literally 'Baths-Baths') for its curative springs and healthy air.

From Baden-Baden, the Schwarzwaldhochstrasse twists and turns its way towards Bühlerhöhe, the top of the ridge which forms the backbone of the northern Black Forest. There are regular parking areas, and from one of them a short walk to the Geroldsau Waterfall is typical of the romantic scenery you can expect from the Black Forest. Bühlerhöhe is the setting for the grand alpine Schlosshotel (castle-hotel) Bühlerhöhe, built just before the First World War and as

impressive a sight as the landscape over which it looks. From here the road clings to the western flank of the ridge, providing magnificent views across the Rhine valley towards France and the Vosges Forest. West of the settlement of Sand there are further well-laid out paths leading through woods to beautiful waterfalls. Sand itself is home to the small Mehliskopf ski resort with cross-country trails and half a dozen lifts. In the summer it offers a rail bobsleigh track. Above it all stands the Mehliskopf lookout tower, built for the pleasure of tourists in 1880.

Further along the road are ski areas at Hundseck and Unterstmatt. Because these sports facilities require access, the Schwarzwaldhochstrasse and its feeder roads are kept clear throughout the winter months. The Hochstrasse now skirts

ABOVE: The famous Trinkhalle, built between 1839 and 1842 for taking the waters in the Kurhaus Spa at Baden-Baden.

the slopes of the area's highest mountain, the 1,164-metre (3,819-ft) Hornisgrinde. There are good paths to the summit from which, naturally, a wonderful view extends in all directions. Be aware however that *grinde* means 'bog' and that the peak has one of the highest annual rainfalls in Germany. You may be happier with the 23-metre (75-ft) high Hornisgrinde lookout tower which sits on its southern slope. Built

in 1910 it began life as a tourist attraction for visitors to the beautiful lake Mummelsee, but was given over to military use from 1938 to 1994.

The Mummelsee is a charming place to break your journey. It's a relic of the last ice age, almost perfectly circular and surprisingly deep at about 17 metres (56 ft) – watch out for the Nix, a shape-changing water spirit said to inhabit its waters.

So it's no surprise that the Brothers Grimm drew on Black Forest folk legends for their famous fairy tales.

It's a popular tourist spot, and if you need to catch a glimpse of the Nix, you can rent a rowing boat. If you would rather leave the crowds behind, the similar Wildsee is an oasis of calm buried deep in the forest a little further south,

about a 1.5-km walk from the road. Continuing on the road you reach Ruhestein, the high point of an age-old mountain pass which crosses the Black Forest from East to West.

Ruhestein means 'Peace Stone' or 'Sanctuary Stone' and the original stone was a boundary marker between the Kingdom of Württemburg and the Grand Duchy of Baden. Nowadays the headquarters of the Northern Black Forest Nature Park is here, and the village's winter sports complex includes a ski jump. For the adventurous, a longish walk in the forest west of Ruhestein leads you to Karlsruher Grat, a rocky outcrop with a *klettersteig* – a ladder of metal rungs fixed into the rock to aid climbers.

It's worth taking a short detour at Ruhestein to visit Allerheiligen where there is a ruined monastery (Allerheiligen means 'All-Saints') and

a very pretty waterfall. But return to Ruhestein or face a long and winding road which does not rejoin the Hochstrasse until much further south. Continuing south from Ruhestein you come to Lotharpfad, and only 250 metres from the road a splendid timber viewing platform, the Lotharaussichtsplattform. Standing on it you are above the trees and get a sense of the vastness of this forested wonderland.

South from here the long road from Allerheiligen, the L402, rejoins the route; and after the village of Kneibis the Black Forest High Road descends at last, following the Forbach stream all the way to Freudenstadt. Nestled on a plateau below the northern Black Forest, Freudenstadt is famed for its clean air and the largest market square in Germany. It's a fitting place to draw breath after such a breathtaking journey.

OPPOSITE: Ruins of the All Saints Abbey near Allerheiligen. The abbey was hit by a bolt of lightening in 1804 after which the stone was plundered for local churches.

TOP: The grand, baroque-style Schlosshotel Bühlerhöhe was opened in 1912, the vision of Hertha Isenbart. It has commanding views over the Rhine Plain and the Vosges.

ABOVE: The enormous market square in Freudenstadt.

The Blue Ridge Parkway

Virginia/North Carolina, USA

Length: 469 miles, 755 km
Start: Afton, VA
Finish: Cherokee, NC
Highlights: Humpback Rocks, Roanoke Gorge, Mabry Mill, Brinegar Cabin, Linn Cove Viaduct, Linville Falls, Oconaluftee Vistor Centre

What makes the Blue Ridge Mountains blue? Apparently it's the haze of isoprene released by the acres of trees which cover the ridge. The Blue Ridge Parkway is perennially the most popular scenic drive in America's National Park system.

Work on the Blue Ridge Parkway (BRP) began in 1935. Like many roads begun during the Great Depression it was built not simply to expand the transport infrastructure but to provide work for the unemployed, in this case at the behest of President Franklin D. Roosevelt. During the Second World War the work was continued by pacifists and other conscientious objectors. The route was finally completed in 1966, apart from a small, five-mile section which finally bridged the gap around Grandfather Mountain in 1987.

This is a long, slow-paced drive through Virginia and North Carolina. Speeds are limited to 45mph, often less, and one of its great pleasures is the view far into the distance. This is something to savour, not to rush past. Commercial vehicles are banned from the BRP, so no one will be tailgating you to hurry up. The road meanders more like a lazy river than an A-to-B expressway. And in the BRP's 469 miles there are at least 194 roadside

viewpoints – an average of more than one every two and a half miles. The Blue Ridge Parkway positively begs you to take your time.

It doesn't much matter which end you start at. From the south, if you set off early enough, you will see the sun rise; from the north the sunset will be ahead of you. The northern entrance is in the Virginia town of Afton at Skyline Drive. Within the first 6 miles you will have passed three viewpoints and arrived at Humpback Rocks, the first of 15 official visitor centres along the route. The Humpback Rocks are a good example of what you can expect throughout the BRP – a

combination of natural and cultural experiences. There are trails through the woods, and the strikingly shaped rocky outcrop of Humpback Mountain stands out above the vast forest canopy, and from it there are views of infinite depth in all directions. Humpback Gap is one of many historic passes which crossed the Blue Ridge, part of the Appalachian Mountain Range. A collection of 19th-century farm buildings and

ABOVE: The entrance to the Blue Ridge Parkway at US-19 on the Haywood/Jackson county line.

RIGHT: Mabry Water Mill at milepost 176.1 has a restored sawmill. Musicians gather here on summer Sundays.

an exhibition explain life here in times gone by. History and nature go hand in hand along the Blue Ridge.

Up ahead around Otter Creek and James River you can see a different kind of route through the mountains. A plan to develop the river as a major trade artery in Virginia, by digging the Kanawha Canal, was ultimately unsuccessful, but you can visit a restored canal lock and read the history of the failed project. Climbing back up the mountains the Parkway passes the Norfolk and Western Railroad, yet another transport route across the Ridge, which was laid down in 1852

and passed through nearby Roanoke. You can walk to the Roanoke Gorge, through which the Roanoke River forces its way.

A few miles short of the border between Virginia and North Carolina is one of the highlights of the trip, Mabry Mill. The wooden buildings of the water-powered mill and their waterside setting are emblematic images of rural America. Built by Ed Mabry at the start of the 20th century it operated as both a cornmill and a sawmill and has been restored to working order. The Blue Ridge Music Center, just the Virginia side of the state line, has daily performances of old-

time music on traditional instruments, and an exhibition tracing the history of the sound to its European and African roots and its continuing influence on more modern music.

Cumberland Knob just across the state line in North Carolina is the point at which construction work first began on this treasured route. A little further south is an amazing survivor of even older times, Brinegar Cabin, built here in 1880 by one Martin Brinegar and still lived in by his widow in the 1930s. Here you really can glimpse the past. At E. B. Jeffress Park, named for a great supporter of the Parkway project when it was first proposed, there are the Cascade Falls which tumble down a steep cliff. It's thanks to Jeffress that there are no tolls throughout the Parkway's length.

At around the 300-mile mark the road seems to take flight, on the Linn Cove Viaduct. This was part of the last section of the BRP to be built. Designed not to damage the ancient environment of Grandfather Mountain around which it snakes, the viaduct is constructed in 153 sections, only one of which is straight. It's an engineering marvel.

There are several viewpoints with trails around Grandfather Mountain, and just to the south of it are the Linville Falls, a series of spectacular waterfalls dropping into a deep gorge. Here, as at many stops on the Parkway, you can get up close to the wonderful diversity of plantlife.

Besides the 174 bridges and viaducts which the BRP crosses, rather more than one every

TOP LEFT: Groundhog Mountain Lookout Tower and split-rail fence is at milepost 188.8.

LEFT: A section of the Blue Ridge Parkway near Lexington, Virginia. The BRP links the Shenandoah National Park to the Great Smoky Mountains National Park.

RIGHT: An outdoor jam and jelly stall in Linville.

3 miles, there are 26 tunnels, all but one of them in the final 140 miles. Three of them come in the space of a little over half a mile as the Parkway descends around and through the flanks of Ferrin Knob.

At Looking Glass Rock there is a trail to Skinny Dip Falls, where as the name suggests the water cascades into a swimming hole. The Rock itself is so called because it is pure granite and glistens after rain. A few miles further on the road reaches Beech Gap, another of the old passes over the Blue Ridge. From here the Parkway now turns north-west for its final 45 miles, climbing steadily to reach its highest point at Richland Balsam, 6,053 ft (1,845 metres) above sea level.

It's a short walk to the summit of Richland Balsam Mountain, but ironically the views are limited by the dense forestry all around. Better views are to be found at Licklog Gap a little further on. Now the road descends gradually more than 3,800 ft (1,158 metres) in the last few miles. The land around here was all Cherokee, and the Oconaluftee Vistor Center tells their story. The Blue Ridge Trail ends soon after, near the town of Cherokee on the Oconaluftee River.

The Blue Ridge Parkway is an immense journey. It travels through time; through native and European American history; and above all through nature – a variety of habitats, trees and shrubs you would be hard-pressed to find together anywhere else. Every viewpoint has a new view; every trail leads somewhere different; every visitor centre offers the chance to stretch your legs, refresh your body and mind, and learn something about the vast land through which you are travelling. As The Eagles said – *Take it Easy*.

LEFT: Linn Cove viaduct, completed in 1983, snakes round Grandfather Mountain in western North Carolina. It was one of the last construction projects on the Parkway.

BELOW: Looking Glass Rock in the Pisgah National Forest is clearly visible from the Parkway.

TOP RIGHT: Known by the Cherokee as 'the river of many cliffs' the Linville River and Falls are fed by headwaters on Grandfather Mountain.

RIGHT: Craggy Pinnacle Tunnel near Asheville, NC, at milepost 364.4. It's followed soon after by one at 365.5, Craggy Flats.

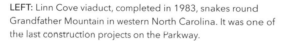

Cabot Trail

Nova Scotia, Canada

Length: 300 km, 185 miles
Start/Finish: Baddeck
Highlights: Margaree Valley, Pleasant Bay, Neil's Harbour, Ingonish, The Gaelic College

Encircling the northern half of Cape Breton island, the route provides exhilarating twists and turns along a rugged coastline, visiting small communities and big seas on the way round.

The Cabot Trail was constructed in 1932 as part of a drive by Nova Scotia politician Angus L. Macdonald to boost tourism on his native island of Cape Breton. Descended from Scottish immigrants, Macdonald promoted Nova Scotia as a little piece of Scotland in Canada – Nova Scotia, after all, means New Scotland in Latin. He accentuated the Scottish heritage in place names such as Aberdeen, Inverness and the Cape Breton Highlands, and encouraged the old Gaelic language and culture. With a name like Cape Breton, the island also has a strong French past, and just off the Cabot Trail you will also encounter Englishtown, with its fish and chip shop.

The Cabot Trail is short enough to be driven in a single day, although your experience will be immeasurably richer if you spend two or more days on the journey. A three- or four-day cycling tour is a popular way of seeing it all at a leisurely pace. Travelling in an anticlockwise direction puts you on the side of the road nearest the sea – best for views, but not so good if you or your passengers are nervous of steep drops. Most people drive clockwise.

The Trail starts and finishes in Baddeck, the nearest thing to a centre of population in rural Victoria County. With a population of just 700, it offers hotel accommodation for another 600. Scottish-born inventor of the telephone Alexander Graham Bell was a resident here, and his experimental hydrofoil broke the marine speed record on nearby Bras d'Or Lake in 1919. The Alexander Graham Bell National Historic Site is in Baddeck.

Leaving Baddeck and heading westwards, the Cabot Trail soon turns north and climbs gently but steadily up through forests over Hunter's Mountain. Eventually it meets the broad valley of the Margaree river and follows it down to the sea at Margaree Harbour. The Margaree Valley boasts excellent fishing and kayaking. This western side of Cape Breton, known as the

OPPOSITE: The Cabot Trail as it turns inland at Cap Rouge.

Acadian Coast, is distinctly French in flavour and you stick close to the water's edge as you pass through the settlements of Grand Étang and Chéticamp.

In Chéticamp you can join whale-watching cruises. Beyond the town you turn inland, leaving the coastal plain and climbing up into the Cape Breton Highlands. There are several trailheads on this stretch, starting points for some of the twenty-six signed trails through the mountains. When the road drops once again to the sea, it is to a coast of a very different character. Steep cliffs drop to narrow, stony beaches, while the road makes its way above them as best it can. Forced inland at one point, it then descends by a dizzying series of hairpin bends to the fishing community of Pleasant Bay, an internationally famous centre for whale-watching.

From Pleasant Bay the Cabot Trail turns away from the Acadian Coast to the eastern side of the island. Cape North is the route's most northerly point and nearby, Dingwall (named after a town in northern Scotland) has a lighthouse with a history. The Trail cuts overland to Neil's Harbour from Cape North; but if you prefer, White Point Road hugs the inlets and bays of the coast and arrives at Neil's Harbour via New Haven Road.

Neil's Harbour is a scattered fishing community first settled by a Frenchman but named after someone of Scottish descent, Neil Maclennan. The Chowder House, on a peninsula jutting into the bay there, is an essential refreshment stop on the Cabot Trail. South from here, on this gentler side of the island, the Trail connects a series of shallow inlets – Black Brook Cove, Mackinnon Cove, Broad Cove and others – with a mixture of weathered rocky shores and sandy beaches. The last of these leads into Ingonish.

Ingonish was where some of the earliest settlers on Cape Breton arrived. Today its population of under thirty is swollen by summer visitors drawn

to its natural beauty and large camp site. Its sandy shores, North Bay and South Bay, are divided by Middle Head, a long narrow spit of land with great footpaths. South Bay has a fine natural harbour protected by two sand bars. If you like your weather wild, go in the winter when the area is regularly battered by northeasterly storms.

Continuing south past more coves, at the aptly named Macdonald's Big Pond, the Cabot Trail turns inland and follows the west bank of the North River. It crosses the peninsula at St Ann's Bay where you will find the Gaelic College, A' Colaisde na Gàidhlig, which was funded by Angus L. Macdonald. From the college it is a fifteen minute drive back to Baddeck where the Cabot Trail ends.

Reflecting French and Scottish roots, and set amidst dramatic mountain and coastal scenery, the Cabot Trail is Canada in miniature. The current historical thinking is that John Cabot, the first European to discover North America, made landfall in Newfoundland rather than Cape Breton. Nevertheless the trail named in his honour is a perfect way to make your own discoveries of the country and the people who settled there.

RIGHT TOP: View from the top of the Skyline hiking trail looking down at the Cabot Trail.

BELOW RIGHT: A large bull moose with velvet antlers photographed in the Cape Breton Highlands National Park.

BELOW FAR RIGHT: Kidston Island lighthouse at the Trail's end opposite Baddeck.

BELOW: White Point Harbour, a few kilometres east of Dingwall at the northern end of the Trail.

The Causeway Coastal Route

Northern Ireland

Length: 120 miles, 190 km
Start: Belfast
Finish: Londonderry
Highlights: Titanic Belfast, Glens of Antrim, Dunluce Castle, Carrick-a-Rede Rope Bridge, Giant's Causeway, Londonderry Walls

For viewers of HBO's global smash *Game of Thrones* parts of this scenic drive around the Northern Irish coast from Belfast to Londonderry will seem very familiar...

The Causeway Coastal Route follows the seashore north from Carrickfergus to Ballycastle where it turns west to Londonderry. The rocky bays, sweeping beaches, high sea cliffs and deep glens which line the coast provide scenic grandeur. The route has urban charms too. Before you leave Belfast, Titanic Belfast is a must-see visitor attraction which tells the story of the world's most famous ship, built in the city.

About forty minutes northeast of Belfast, beyond Carrickfergus's well preserved Norman fortress, you reach the Islandmagee peninsula. Here is The Gobbins, a strenuous walk that traverses the rugged basalt cliffs. The tubular and suspension bridges, tunnels, caves and steep steps which make up the path are accessible only via a guided tour. Safety helmets are provided, and you will need stout footwear.

Turning northwest, the next significant castle stop is Glenarm Castle, the ancestral home of the McDonnells, Earls of Antrim. The Castle is

occasionally open to the public but the well-tended, 18th-century walled garden is always open from Easter to September and offers fine views of the Castle and sea beyond.

The route also takes in several locations which have featured prominently in the hugely popular *Game of Thrones* fantasy television series. Belfast has been an important hub for the film crew and an entire *Game of Thrones* tourism industry has grown up around the global hit. The conservation village of Cushendun sits at the foot of Glendun, one of the nine Glens of Antrim; and you may recognize the Cushendun sea caves as the place where the red priestess Melisandre created a shadow assassin.

Beyond Ballycastle, near Ballintoy, is a short walk over a bridge to the tiny Carrick-a-Rede island, a Site of Special Scientific Interest. The bridge is only 20 metres long but the 30-metre (100-ft) drop to the waves below may make it seem much longer. Oh, and it's made of rope. It's nerve-shreddingly wobbly.

To steady your nerves, continue as the road heads west to Bushmills. Here, Ireland's oldest working distillery has been producing whiskey on site since 1608 and both guided tours and tutored tastings are offered to visitors. Nearby, perched on sea cliffs, is Dunluce Castle, whose romantic ruins will tug on your heart strings. It has a long and bloody history dating back to at least 1513. Naturally, it reports its fair share of ghosts and even a banshee. Not that Dunluce

TOP: Carrick-a-Rede rope bridge, Ballintoy.

ABOVE: Cushendun village lies across the bay from Castle Carra.

OPPOSITE: The striking ruins of Dunluce Castle.

needs any supernatural involvement to create drama. On one particularly stormy night in 1639, according to legend, the castle kitchens fell into the sea killing all the staff bar the kitchen boy.

A short detour inland from here brings you to Gracehill House, where in the 18th century the Stuart family planted an avenue of beech trees to create an imposing approach to their stately home. Now fully grown, the trees form a green tunnel known as the Dark Hedges, familiar to *Game of Thrones* fans as part of the Kingsroad which runs from Kings Landing, past Winterfell, all the way to Castle Black on the Wall.

The jewel in the crown of the Causeway Coastal Route is the Giant's Causeway between Bushmills and Portrush, an Area of Outstanding Beauty and Northern Ireland's only World Heritage Site. Some 60 million years ago, volcanic eruptions resulted in the creation of approximately 40,000 polygonal basalt columns on the shoreline. Best viewed at dawn, before the crowds arrive, the Causeway is an otherworldly location which has fostered several, colourful genesis myths.

After the old coastal resort of Portrush, and the modern university town of Coleraine, the Causeway Coastal Route reaches its destination in the noble city of Londonderry. Close to the border with the Republic of Ireland, this place has seen more than its share of conflict, as a walk round the well-preserved 17th-century defensive walls will show you.

Londonderry (or Derry as it is known to Irish nationalists) has a fine old city centre, and is approached from the east by three fine bridges. The central cantilever span of the 1984 Foyle Bridge is the longest in Ireland; the Craigavon Bridge is an unusual double-decker opened in 1933, originally carrying a railway line on its lower deck; and the graceful Peace Bridge was built in 2011 to encourage cyclists and pedestrians to move freely between the unionist and nationalist communities of the city.

However you enter the city, take time to reflect on the beauty and drama through which the Coastal Route has transported you. It's a shorter and duller journey back to Belfast on the A6 with nothing at all to remind you of Westeros.

RIGHT: Ballintoy Harbour, used in *Game of Thrones* as the Iron Islands' Lordsport Harbour, the scene of Theon Greyjoy's homecoming.

BELOW LEFT: The unmistakeable Giants Causeway. With an estimated million visitors a year it is wise to pick your moment to visit. As there is a public right of way to the basalt columns, it can be accessed at any time, night or day.

BELOW: These ancient beech trees were planted in 1775 for the approach to Gracehill House. Known as the Dark Hedges they line the busy Bregagh Road. However, due to its popularity the road was pedestrianized in 2017.

Cotswold Market Towns

England

Length: 60 miles, 96 km
Start: Chipping Norton
Finish: Stow-on-the-Wold
Highlights: Chipping Norton, Rollright Stones, Moreton in the Marsh, Chipping Campden, Broadway Tower, Broadway, Stanton, Stanway, The Slaughters, Stow-on-the-Wold

The Cotswold villages are quintessentially English and this tour meanders along some of the smaller roads with enticing country pubs a serious distraction to the journey.

The Cotswold Hills stretch from the Vale of Evesham in the north, to beyond Tetbury, south of Gloucester, at the south-western end. Formed from Jurassic limestone, the rolling hills have been sheep pasture for centuries and many of the grand, stone-built country houses were funded with profits from the 16th- and 17th-century wool trade.

It has been designated an Area of Outstanding Natural Beauty (AONB) since the 1960s, which has helped preserve many of the picture-perfect villages that dot the countryside. It is an area criss-crossed with small roads where getting lost is all part of the charm; because then tourists can stumble upon their own personal discoveries. In the Cotswolds delightful villages are everywhere.

Our route takes the driver through five key market towns in the Cotswolds, each with

LEFT: The grand neoclassical town hall at Chipping Norton, built in 1824 from Cotswold stone.

RIGHT: The King's Men stone circle at the Rollright Stones. There are three Neolithic and Bronze Age monuments in all.

their own distinct differences, but all unified by glorious Cotswold stone. The start point is Chipping Norton in Oxfordshire, (Chipping comes from the Olde English *ceping* for market place) the first of four English counties we'll notch up in a short space of time. Those on a UK tour, arriving from the direction of Oxford will probably want to allow for a stop to visit Blenheim Palace which is just off the A44 heading north-west from the city and en route.

Chipping Norton is perched on the eastern flank of the Cotswolds and athough most of the three-story townhouses in the centre of town are older, the single stand-out building is the Bliss Tweed Mill built in 1872 in the valley below. However, we head north out of town, past the Blue Boar pub in the High Street (on the left), taking the first exit of three at a complicated mini-roundabout at the bottom of the hill. This takes us to the A3400 and a left-turn needed towards the much signposted Rollrights. The neolithic Rollright Stones are the first possible diversion, a circle of embedded stones dating back 4,000 years and a burial chamber, the Whispering Knights, 5,000 years. Alternatively, you could make a right-turn and head to the famous Hook Norton brewery – a site of pilgrimage for bearded men fond of real ale.

Continuing on the A3400 would take us further into Warwickshire and on to Shipston-on-Stour, which gives a real contrast between a typical old Warwickshire market town (not dissimilar from Stratford upon Avon) and those we're about to visit. Instead we take a left turn at Long Compton, through Barton on the Heath untill we reach the A44 and onwards to Moreton-in-Marsh,

TOP: The 400-year-old Market Hall in Chipping Campden is owned by the National Trust.

RIGHT: St James Church and the East Banqueting Hall in Chipping Campden. Campden House was destoryed by fire during the English Civil War and today only the Banqueting House remains. Owned by the Landmark Trust it is available for hire and sleeps six.

our second market town stop and popular because of its main line railway station. It's one of the few stations in England with Japanese signage thanks to the volume of tourists.

After Moreton, continue on the A44 through Bourton-on-the-Hill with its old cottages tight by the busy road. Imagine how difficult it would have been to traverse this steep hill with a wagon and horses at the time they were built. Beyond Bourton there's a right turn onto the B4479 and if you like an arboretum, there's one at Batsford, before you meander north to the B4305 and take a left to Chipping Campden.

Chipping Campden is the endpoint of the 102-mile Cotswold Way walking path and full of splendid Jacobean buildings and the unique Market Hall preserved by the National Trust on the High Street. From Chipping Campden you can head north and divert to the famous Hidcote Manor Gardens (National Trust), or south and divert to Snowshill (National Trust) or Broadway Tower, which is the kind of stark stone tower you would imagine a Thomas Hardy heroine standing on, if only he had written his novels a little further north. It is in fact a folly created by Capability Brown in 1794, and like Hidcote, linked to the Arts and Crafts movement.

From here you descend into Broadway on the A44 and your fourth county of the day, the very south-east corner of Worcestershire. 'Jewel of the Cotswolds' Broadway was once the domain of the Mercian kings in the 10th century and by the time of the Domesday Book in 1086 was known as 'Bradweia'. Today it boasts genteel art galleries, tea shoppes and elegant hotels – and it does have a very broad main street.

Head out of Broadway on the B4632, which is a continuation of the main street. Two miles out of town, start looking for signposts on the left to Stanton. Stanton is the archetypal Cotswold village with its own Jacobean manor house

TOP: Batsford Park, near Moreton-in-Marsh, was once the home of Nancy Mitford.

ABOVE AND RIGHT: Stanway Gate and Stanway House from the churchyard. Gloucestershire folk artist Johnny Coppin has set many of the local poets – including Laurie Lee and Ivor Gurney – to music and his songs are an essential soundtrack.

and a bucolic main street that heads uphill to a dead end at the popular 17th-century Mount pub. There are so many beguiling country pubs on this route that you will need to develop strong willpower to resist them all. From the top of Stanton village it's a U-turn; go back down the main street and then take a left turn onto a minor road to Stanway. If it's a Sunday afternoon in summer you may be lucky enough to see cricket being played on an idyllic ground in parkland to the right of the road. There is a vintage, thatched pavilion donated to the club by J. M. Barrie (author of *Peter Pan*) and a little further along, the home of the club's landlord, Lord Wemyss, the Grade I-listed Stanway House. Further still is the magnificent Stanway Gate (circa 1630) celebrated by World War One poet and Gloucestershire lad Ivor Gurney who wrote, 'in hidden state lies Stanway Gate and Stanway

BELOW: The lower end of Broadway lightly dusted with snow.

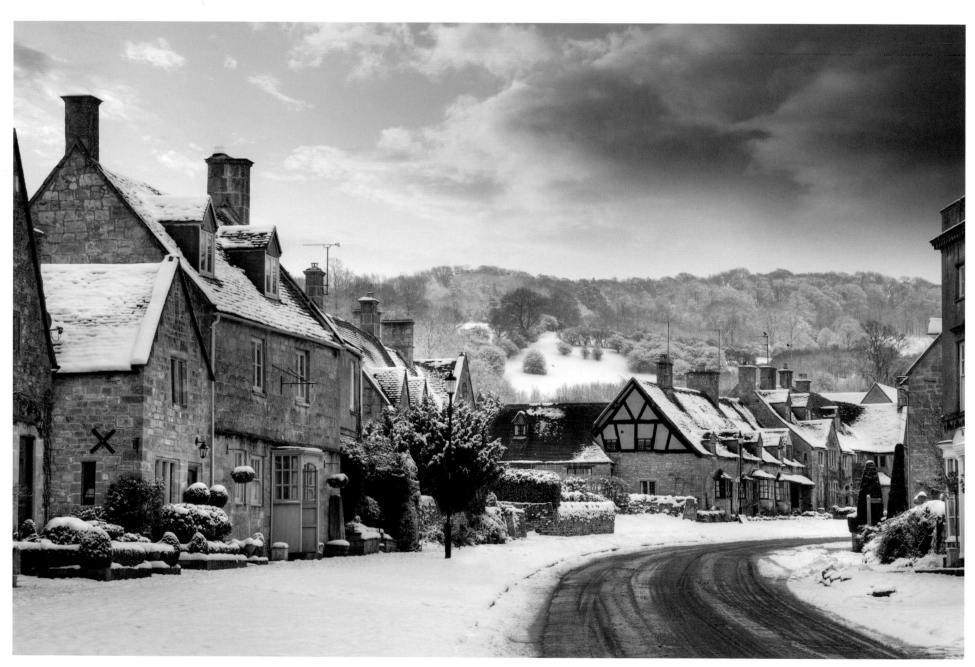

Woods beyond.' It is only a few hundred yards till a left turn is needed onto the B4077 which can take you to our fifth and final market town of Stow-on-the-Wold. Except we will divert to the Slaughters first. After about 4 miles and the other side of the village of Ford, which has a sharp-angled turn by another alluring pub – The Plough – there is a wooded crossroads with a signpost to the Cotswold Farm Park and The Slaughters.

Upper Slaughter is nice, but it is the village of Lower Slaughter with its carefully channelled roadside stream running through the heart of the village that will fill your camera's memory card. Nearby Bourton-on-the-Water is the better known of these rural village idylls and the one blessed with coachloads of tourists in summer.

After Lower Slaughter it is less than half a mile to the Roman Road, the Fosse Way, which will take you the 4 miles to Stow-on-the-Wold; although today the road is better known as the A429. Stow, like all the other market towns is a hive of rural gentility stocked with art galleries, antique shops, charming hotels and irresistible pubs. And at last you can go inside, knowing that a second pint is not out of the question.

Dempster Highway

Yukon Territory, Canada

Length: 736 km, 457 miles
Start: Dawson City
Finish: Inuvik
Highlights: North Fork Pass, Chapman Lake, Ogilvie Mountains, Eagle Plains, Arctic Circle, Fort Macpherson, Mackenzie River, Beaufort Sea

This challenging route through Canada's arctic northwest should be savoured along every majestic wilderness kilometre of its length. Take extra provisions; take extra fuel; take a week.

Dawson City, at the meeting of the Klondike and Yukon rivers, makes a good base at which to prepare yourself for the Dempster Highway. It was the centre of the Klondike goldrush for a three-year period in the 1890s, during which the population rose from a few hundred to 40,000, then fell back to 8,000. It's now less than 1,500 and still the largest town you'll see until the end of your Dempster Highway adventure. Enjoy its historic atmosphere and stock up on everything you think you might need for your journey. There are only two supply centres between here and the end of the Dempster.

Head 39 km east from Dawson on the Klondike Highway until you see an unassuming sign announcing Yukon Highway 5 to Fort Macpherson and Inuvik. Turn left here. This is it, and the gas station at this junction is the last for 369 km. From here the Dempster follows the

North Klondike River upstream for some 70 km until it veers westwards into the Tombstone mountain range. There's a campsite here and, a little further on as the road climbs towards North Fork Pass, a viewpoint by the roadside where you may stop and wonder why the dark Tombstone peaks were so named.

North Fork Pass, below Trapper Mountain to the east, is the highest point on the highway at 1,298 m (4,229 ft). Beyond it the road crosses the Blackstone uplands, a plateau of low growing heather and shrubs. Watch out for the Joe and Annie Henry memorial to a couple who worked as trappers here before the Dempster Highway was built. They advised surveyors of the route.

The Dempster Highway crosses a rare bridge to join the Blackstone River. On the left is Chapman Lake, with information boards which remind you why the road was built and named. The route

was regularly used at the beginning of the 20th century by patrols of the North West Mounted Police. In 1910, in bad weather and rough terrain, one patrol got lost. Corporal William Dempster became a national hero after undertaking the sad task of discovering their bodies just a few miles short of shelter. Chapman Lake also boasts an airstrip, of which – beware – the road you are driving on forms a part.

Eventually the road pulls away from Blackstone River, crossing a pass to join Engineer Creek which it follows downstream until it meets the Ogilvie River. Engineer Creek is named after the 3rd Canadian Engineers who built the bridge over the Ogilvie. The Dempster now follows the Ogilvie for 50 km as it gathers meltwater and rainfall from the surrounding Ogilvie mountains, before striking up into those mountains. The landscape is covered in stunted trees, surviving as best they can in this high, harsh environment.

PREVIOUS PAGE: A view of the distant Ogilvie Mountains in Tombstone Territorial Park.

TOP: With a loose gravel surface for much of the Dempster's length, a 4X4 with a large fuel tank is essential in winter.

ABOVE: Breaking down in this kind of scenery might turn your road trip from a cheery adventure into a remake of *The Revenant*. There is little or no cell phone coverage on the Dempster.

Finding its way across this terrain the road arrives, on a slight rise, at the midpoint of the Dempster Highway – Eagle Plains, with gas, mechanical repair services and a hotel. If you need anything, get it here. The next fuel stop is 180 km further on.

It was the discovery of oil in this area in 1959 which prompted the construction of the Highway; but work had only got as far as the Blackstone uplands when in 1962 the extraction of the oil proved unviable and construction was halted. It started up again in 1970 and was at last completed in 1978. Although the loose stone and dust surface of the road may seem primitive, a great deal of engineering skill went into the building of the road. In particular, care had to be taken that the heat generated by traffic on the surface did not start to melt the permafrost underneath. The road therefore sits on an insulating layer of gravel up to 2.4m (8 ft) thick.

From this high plain the road drops down to cross Eagle River on another fine bridge before climbing again to run alongside the Eagle Plains airstrip. A further 27 km beyond the bridge, the Dempster Highway finally crosses the Arctic Circle, the only highway in Canada to do so. A helpful sign helps you prove with a selfie that you've done it too.

The Highway presses on with few bends, in a way more associated with desert roads than mountains. The terrain may look flat and tempting to go walkabout on, but it is soft and wet, pockmarked with lakes and waterholes, and treacherous underfoot, all the more so in snow or rain. Depending on the weather for your trip you may well understand how a patrol of experienced Mounties got lost, and how

TOP RIGHT: The Northern Lights – Aurora Borealis – over the Ogilvie Mountains.

RIGHT: A roadside marker announces your arrival in the Arctic Circle and prompts a photo opportunity.

impressive the construction of the Dempster is over such ground.

North of the Arctic Circle, after crossing Sheep Creek and Rock River, you climb a little more steeply up to Wright Pass, which marks the boundary between Yukon and the North West Territories. It's a good moment to stop and look back across the infinity of mountain ranges through which you have come. It's also time to change your watches – set them an hour ahead to Mountain Time if travelling north, or an hour back to Pacific if heading south. You're now more than 500 km from Dawson City, and still 270 km to go.

The road twists through hills and over plateaux now, with the Richardson Mountains to the north, until it comes to the natural barrier of the Peel River. No bridge spans the Peel; instead, the MV *Abraham Francis* ferries traffic back and forth between June and October. Between November and April the river is frozen solid enough to bear the weight of vehicles, making what they call an ice bridge. But there are times before June and after mid October when the ferry can't make the crossing and the ice, either thawing or yet to freeze completely, can't carry the load. At such times Fort Macpherson on the far side of the river is cut off from the south.

It was only a few miles from Fort Macpherson that William Dempster found the bodies of the lost patrol. Their graves and a monument are here. The small town, population around 750, began life as an important outpost of the Hudson Bay Company. Its motto is 'Take What You Need' and Fort Macpherson is the last trading post on the Dempster Highway before Inuvik.

Just beyond the town, another ferry, the MV *Louis Cardinal*, crosses the vast Mackenzie River. Across the Arctic Red River, which joins the Mackenzie here, you can see the clifftop houses of the village of Tsiigehtchic, only accessible by

another ferry from this point. Here, too, an ice bridge functions during the winter.

Just downstream from here the Mackenzie, the longest river in Canada, splits into the myriad streams of the Mackenzie Delta, second only to the Mississippi in scale, before emptying into the Beaufort Sea. The Dempster skirts the delta's eastern edge passing Inuvik's airport and Jak Territorial Park, a serviced campsite with a high wooden observation tower from which to get an overview of this final landscape of your journey.

Inuvik, built on permafrost, was conceived as a new town in the 1950s because the old administrative centre of the region, Aklavik, is vulnerable to floodwaters. With a population of over 3,000 it is by far the largest settlement on the Dempster, with resources and facilities to match. It hosts a sunrise festival in January (at the end of 30 days of continuous night), a traditional games and music festival around Easter and

an annual arts festival in July. Inuvik also boasts America's most northerly mosque, which was built in Winnipeg in 2010 and transported to Inuvik by truck and barge – a remarkable act of devotion.

From Inuvik in late 2017 a new road opened extending the Dempster's Arctic reach a further 138 km to the village of Tukyaktuk on the coast. Tuk, as it's known for short, is a former centre of caribou and whale hunting with a good natural harbour and an unusually dense concentration of periglacial ice hills called pingos. For now however, stop a while in Inuvik and think about how far you've come, before turning the car around and heading for home.

ABOVE: Journey's end at Inuvik. Provisions are expensive in such a remote location, so stock up before you go.

OPPOSITE: The warmer, drier months may be the easiest time to drive, but beware of mosquitos and black flies.

The Garden Route

South Africa

Length: 800 km, 500 miles
Start: Port Elizabeth
Finish: Cape Town
Highlights: Storms River, Gansbaai, Hermanus, Cape Peninsula

Sandwiched between mountains and the Indian Ocean, this spectacular 800-km drive encompasses some diverse landscapes including stunning beaches, thick forests, game reserves, vineyards, rivers, heady mountain passes and cliff-top ocean vistas.

Be sure to begin this drive from the East, driving towards the setting sun, to make the most of the spectacular evening views you will encounter along the way. The region's amazing culinary scene is an essential part of the journey, too. Best of all, this drive is a year-round proposition with temperatures rarely dropping below 10°C or rising above 30°C.

Your start is Port Elizabeth, known as 'the friendly city', and before you set off, an outing to Addo Elephant Park for a guided evening game drive is well worth a trip. During the day make the most of some of the stunning beaches. If you are after boardwalk bars and restaurants head for Summerstrand; for more peace and tranquillity try the stunning Sardinia Bay.

Leaving Port Elizabeth on the N2, head west through the Tsitsikamma forest towards Knysna. Surfers will want to stop at the legendary Jeffreys Bay surf break ('J-Bay') whilst Storms River should be an obligatory stop for its immense natural

beauty and the sheer wildness of the crashing seas, precipitous cliffs and breathtaking views. An indicator of the beauty of this area is the year-long waiting list to walk the 5-day Otter Trail that skirts this section of coastline.

Soon afterwards you reach Plettenberg Bay and Knysna, which are both good stops for an overnight stay. A detour inland via the Outeniqua Pass takes you across switchback passes and through more stunning vistas before reaching

the feather capital of the world, Oudshoorn. Famous for its ostrich farming, it is also home to the maze-like Cango Caves. The caves span 4 km of underground caverns and tunnels. After this detour, head back towards the coast and on to Cape L'Agulhas, the most southerly tip of Africa.

OPPOSITE: The rugged splendour of Gordon's Bay.

BELOW: A stone monument at Cape L'Agulhas marks the southernmost tip of the African continent and the dividing line between Atlantic and Indian oceans (view looking out to sea).

From L'Agulhas follow the coast road towards Gansbaai, renowned for its great white shark population. The awe-inspiring predators are drawn to these waters by the 60,000 cape fur seals, which ply the waters of shark alley between Dyer Island and Geyser Rock; making Gansbaai one of the world's best spots for swimming with great white sharks, all be it in the safety of a cage! A little further down the coast you find Hermanus, the whale capital of South Africa and probably one of the best places in the world to

see these giants of the sea whilst still standing on land. The annual whale festival is held at the end of September.

Make sure to hug the coastline along Clarence Drive as you leave Hermanus and the views will not disappoint. This final stretch of the drive is arguably the most spectacular, driving past numerous nature reserves displaying the unique fynbos vegetation, found nowhere else in the world. Take the opportunity to stop for a night

and indulge in the fantastic wines from the copious vineyards along this section of the route – make sure you have somewhere to stay before getting back to the wheel!

As you drive round the coastal pass through Rooi-Els and into the town of Gordon's Bay, you are greeted with views of False Bay and across to Table Mountain and the 'Mother City' of Cape Town. Taking the coastal road down Baden Powell Drive you will pass near the township

of Khayelitsha, a reminder of the legacy left by apartheid. You are certain to see locals fishing from the long windy beach that stretches the length of False Bay.

Finally, reaching the surf village of Muizenburg, you can take the long and beautiful route round the Cape Peninsula, detouring into the Cape of Good Hope, originally thought to be the dividing point between the Indian and Atlantic Oceans – the meeting of currents is now known

to fluctuate between here and l'Agulhas. Be careful of the infamous Cape Baboons, they won't think twice about stealing food from an unattended car, or even a handbag! Make your way past the picturesque suburbs of Kommejie, Noordhoek, Hout Bay, Llandudno, Camps Bay and Greenpoint before ending your journey with a well-deserved drink at the elegant Victoria and Albert hotel on Cape Town's waterfront.

LEFT: A wooden boardwalk leading to Cape L'Agulhas Lighthouse.

TOP: The New Harbour at Hermanus is a great place to embark on a whale watching trip.

ABOVE: Chacma baboons gleefully customize a parked car in Clarence Drive, Gordon's Bay. Careful where you park!

La Grande Corniche

France

Length: 30 km, 19 miles
Start: Nice
Finish: Menton
Highlights: Villefranche-sur-Mer, Col de Villefranche, La Turbie, Èze-Bord-de-Mer, Col d'Èze, Menton

There are three corniche roads between Nice and Menton on the French Riviera: La Grande, La Moyenne and La Basse or L'Inférieure. Arguably, as the highest of the three, La Grande has the best views. Irrefutably, it is the only one to have been built by order of Napoleon.

Carved into the mountains above the Mediterranean coast, all three link Nice, the capital of the Côte d'Azur, and Menton, the more sedate town on the Italian border. The Grande Corniche is the classic Riviera drive but both the Moyenne and Basse Corniche have many plus points.

The Basse or Lower Corniche hugs the shoreline and links luxurious seaside resorts such as Villefranche-sur-Mer, Beaulieu-sur-Mer, Èze-Bord-de-Mer, Cap d'Ail and the millionaires' playground that is the Principality of Monaco. Offering easy access to many of the area's best beaches, it is also one of the busiest. Consequently, when the traffic is heavy, it can feel more like a commute than a wind-in-the-hair drive. Albeit a commute through some of Europe's most glamorous real estate.

This is not just a modern problem. By the 1900s, the burgeoning popularity of the Riviera, particularly among the Russian and European nobility, meant that traffic on the Lower Corniche

RIGHT: The Grand Corniche soars above the coast while the Basse Corniche snakes around the shoreline below.

BELOW: A view of Villefranche-sur-Mer on the Côte d'Azur.

was already a problem. Sensing the economic benefits of more efficient transport links, Prince Albert of Monaco and Albert Figuiera, mayor of the picturesque village of Èze, contributed to the construction of the Moyenne Corniche. The Moyenne features many fine views. The section from Col de Villefranche to just before the tunnel on the aptly named Avenue Bella Vista has amazing panoramas of Beaulieu, Cap Ferrat, Nice and Cap d'Antibes.

However, running at an average height of 500 metres (1,640 ft) above the sea, it is the Grande Corniche that gives drivers the furthest views. Its twists and bends also give the most driving pleasure. Its origins have little do with enjoyment and more to do with military conquest. Napoleon Bonaparte ordered its construction in order to facilitate his Italian campaign in 1796.

Little Boney, as the English referred to him, was following in the footsteps of a more ancient soldier. Large sections of the Grande Corniche were built over the Via Julia Augusta, an old Roman route. Julia was the wife of the Emperor Augustus who subdued the local Ligurian tribes people between 25 and 14 BC. A 35-metre (115-ft) high colonnade, the Trophée des Alpes, was erected in the hilltop town of La Turbie to commemorate the victory of Augustus. Partially restored, the colonnade still dominates the town's skyline. Along with the medieval streets of the historic centre, the Trophée des Alpes makes La Turbie a popular stop on the road from Nice to Menton.

La Turbie also features in Hitchcock's 1955 film *To Catch A Thief* in which Grace Kelly and Cary Grant drive through the village. Slightly more recently, in 1995, the Bond film *GoldenEye*

BELOW LEFT: Èze, which is located on the Moyenne Corniche. The beach beyond is at St Jean-Cap-Ferrat.

BELOW: The medieval village of La Turbie.

BOTTOM: Monte Carlo's casino viewed from below the hairpin on the ridiculously tight Monaco Grand Prix circuit. Nelson Piquet once described it as, 'like cycling round your bathroom'.

made good use of the dramatic scenery on the Grande Corniche around the Col d'Èze mountain pass. Car manufacturers are also well aware that the road provides a setting in which their cars can shine.

It is perfectly feasible to drive all three Corniche routes in one day. They are all approximately 30 km long. Many recommend the Moyenne from Menton to Nice in the morning followed by the return journey via the Grande later in the day. That way, the sun will always be at your back.

There are plenty of roads linking all three and locals zip up and down them in order to reach their preferred bistro, beach or bijou shopping opportunity as efficiently as possible. Their example is worth following. It would seem a shame to drive the Grande and not pop down for a stroll at the vertiginous Botanical Garden at Èze.

Equally, no Formula 1 fan should resist the temptation to nip into Monaco and follow at least some of the race circuit around the streets of the Principality. The opulent and fabled Monte-Carlo casino may be of interest to others. A long winning streak at the tables here might just raise enough money for a down-payment on one of the yachts in the marina.

By contrast, Menton is less flashy but not without its quieter charms. The French and Italians would both lay claim to having the best cuisine in the world. Menton's position on the border and its increasingly fêted restaurant scene mean that visitors have lots of opportunity to sample both styles of cooking and make up their own minds.

TOP RIGHT: Baie des Fourmis at Beaulieu-sur-Mer.

RIGHT: Close to the Italian border, Menton is towered over by the 17th-century basilica of St Michel Archange.

The Great Glen

Scotland

Length: 173 miles, 278 km
Start: Glasgow
Finish: Inverness
Highlights: Loch Lomond, Glencoe, Caledonian Canal, Urquhart Castle

The A82 from Glasgow to Inverness delivers film locations, iconic lochs, dramatic castles and bloody legends. Linking Scotland's most populous city and its fastest growing conurbation, in a little over four hours the journey takes you from the West Coast to the East Coast and from the Lowlands to the Highlands.

The Great Glen is the geological fault line which splits the Highlands of Scotland from the country's Far North. This route drives its entire length and features several fortified sites that tell the story of relatively more recent, dramatic episodes in Scotland's history. The highlights start just north of Glasgow as the road winds along the shores of Loch Lomond and through the Trossachs National Park. This busy area has been immortalized in the folk song 'The Bonnie Banks of Loch Lomond'. At first listening, it is a romantic song of parted lovers. Darker interpretations suggest the lyrics concern the bloody retribution that followed the 1745 Jacobite rebellion.

North of Tyndrum, the scenery rapidly becomes more wild with windswept moors and icy lochans leading to craggy mountains. After the desolate Rannoch moor, the road dips into atmospheric Glencoe, surrounded by some of the best mountain walks and climbs in the country. Infamously, it was the site of the massacre of the Macdonalds by the Campbells. More recently, it was used as a location for the Bond film *Skyfall*.

Crossing the confluence of Loch Linnhe and Loch Leven, the A82 continues north through Fort William and past the bulk of Ben Nevis, the UK's highest mountain. Fort William is at the beginning of the Great Glen and along with Fort Augustus in the middle and Fort George, north of Inverness, the former garrison town played an important strategic role in various attempts to impose control on the Highlands.

The 66-mile (106-km) road along the Great Glen starts at Loch Linnhe and progresses past Loch Lochy, Loch Oich and the iconic Loch Ness. All four are linked by the Caledonian Canal which emerges into Beauly Firth by Inverness. While looking for the mythical monster of Loch Ness has its fans, your time may be spent more gainfully by strolling along Neptune's Staircase, a series of eight locks linking Loch Linnhe and the canal. If you must try to see Nessie, the romantic ruins of Urquhart Castle provide a good vantage point.

Inverness, also known as the Gateway to the Highlands, was, they used to say, where you heard the best spoken English in the United Kingdom, because there it was learned carefully as a second language; Scots Gaelic was in the 19th century the birth tongue of its population. If you didn't find the Loch Ness Monster, you have a better chance of spotting pods of bottlenose dolphins which are permanent residents in nearby Moray Firth, the estuary at the eastern end of your journey.

LEFT: A converted Scottish fishing boat moored at Cullochy Loch on the Caledonian Canal.

RIGHT: No trip to the Great Glen could be complete without a visit to Urquhart Castle.

The Great Ocean Road

Victoria, Australia

Length: 243 km, 151 miles
Start: Melbourne
Finish: Warrnambool
Highlights: Anglesea, Split Point Lighthouse, Apollo Bay, Great Otway National Park, The Twelve Apostles, London Arch

A drive along the south coast of Victoria takes you through lush rainforest, across towering cliffs and along surfing beaches to die for. The Great Ocean Road is steeped in history too, and the fertile coastal land is rich in local produce.

Australian troops returning from their role in the First World War built the original ocean road in the 1920s. The project had two aims – firstly to give the men purpose and income after the trauma of frontline service; and secondly to link the scattered communities of the coast, which until then had been reachable only by boat or overland by the roughest of tracks through the bush. The construction crews worked by hand with the most basic of tools – pick, shovel and dynamite – to carve out a precarious route on which some lost their lives.

When the road was completed in 1932, it was dedicated as a memorial to fallen Australian soldiers. At 243 km in length it remains the largest war memorial in the world. The underlying geology includes sections of crumbly sandstone and the road has been blocked on several occasions by landslides – most recently

in 2011. Water erosion by the sea and torrential rain of frequent storms also undermined the route from time to time. In 1960, a stretch of the road near Princetown was washed away.

It remains today a drive requiring considerable concentration, a good argument for taking frequent breaks from the wheel for refreshment of both body and mind. The route runs from Torquay, just outside Melbourne, westwards to Allansford on the edge of Warrnambool. Leaving Torquay on the B100 the road heads inland at first before sweeping down to join the coast for the first time at Anglesea. This is one of Australia's premium surfing coasts and Anglesea

PREVIOUS PAGE: The Twelve Apostles (don't count them).

ABOVE: The beautiful sandy beach of Apollo Bay.

LEFT: A koala bear takes refuge in a eucalyptus tree in the Great Otway National Park.

OPPOSITE: Tree ferns line a boadwalk through a section of the Great Otway National Park.

has the first of several fine surfing beaches along the Great Ocean Road.

Originally called Swampy Creek before a wise change of name in 1884, Anglesea has grown up around the tidal estuary of the Anglesea River to become a popular resort for Melbournian families. Besides its beach and creek it is famed for the population of wild kangaroos which keep the grass down on its golf course.

Following the coast southwest, the Road reaches the twin communities of Aireys Inlet and Fairhaven, divided by Paincalac Creek. On one side of the creek, Fairhaven boasts a magnificent surf beach which, at 6 km, is the longest along the Great Ocean Road. But this schizophrenic coastline, the Surf Coast, has another name, the Shipwreck Coast. Aireys Inlet with its rocky shore boasts one of the Great Ocean Road's iconic images, the Split Point lighthouse, built in 1891 and still using its original giant Fresnel lens to warn ships of danger. The Fairhaven Surf Lifesaving Club and the Split Point lighthouse together show the dangers to human life which this beautiful coastline presents.

As if to illustrate the point, Lorne – the next town on the route – sits on Loutitt Bay, named after a sea captain who sheltered from bad weather there while trying to salvage the cargo of a wrecked ship. Captain Loutitt's ship was the *Apollo*, from which Apollo Bay, the next town on the itinerary, takes its name. Apollo Bay has its roots in the whaling industry, and despite the activities of the past, whales still come to the area to raise their young in its warm waters. Today the town boasts a Coastal Reserve and considers itself the seafood capital of the Great Ocean Road, a tempting interruption to your journey.

Soon after Apollo Bay the road turns away from the sea to cross the Cape Otway. Otway Point is the most southerly in the region and has given its name to the vast Great Otway National Park,

an amalgamation of many smaller National Reserves. The GONP covers all the coast of the Great Ocean Road as well as considerable areas inland. Encompassing virtually every kind of habitat from sea cliffs to mountain ranges it is an area of unparalleled biodiversity and great natural beauty. It is an important area for birds and particularly rich in fungi, including the pale white Ghost Fungus which glows in the dark.

As you cross Cape Otway a side road leads south to the very tip, where you can visit Cape Otway Lighthouse. Seas are treacherous here where the Bass Strait meets the Southern Ocean. But since the lighthouse was built in 1848, eight more ships have been wrecked on the shores of Cape Otway. West of the Cape and beyond the help of the Otway Lighthouse the schooner *Joanna* was wrecked in 1843, giving its name to the river and small community above which the Great Ocean Road now passes. Joanna's west-facing beach is noted by surfers for its powerful swell.

From Joanna the Great Ocean Road becomes the Great Forest Road as it climbs steadily inland above the Joanna River to Lavers Hill, once an important centre for timber operations and now a well-placed centre for exploring the western GONP in more detail. Here the vegetation is dense and at Melba Gully, off the road which leads from Lavers Hill back toward the sea, you can walk on trails through unspoilt rainforest. Because of its position in the bowl of the Joanna River it has been spared the destruction which bush fires have brought to much of the surrounding woodland.

The Great Ocean Road now runs along inland but parallel to the sea. Where it crosses the Gellibrand River you have the chance to turn left onto the Old Ocean Road, the original route and now little more than a wide dirt track, which follows the river to the sea at Princetown. There the Old is reunited with the Great. Between Princetown and Port Campbell

the Great Ocean Road runs above spectacular cliffs and one of the highlights of the route, the Twelve Apostles.

The Apostles are limestone stacks left isolated in the sea after the erosion of the cliffs of which they were once a part. There were only ever nine of them in fact, and one collapsed in 2005. The survivors are being eroded by the sea at the rate of around 2cm a year; but so are the cliffs behind them, so new Apostles may emerge to replace any more that topple.

There are more remarkable limestone formations beyond Port Campbell, including the London Arch. It used to be two arches and was known as London Bridge, to which it did bear an uncanny resemblance, until in 1990 the shoreside arch collapsed leaving two tourists stranded on the remaining section of the 'bridge'.

TOP: The Flagstaff Hill Maritime Museum and Village at Warrnambool.

ABOVE: London Arch, now minus its second span.

ABOVE RIGHT: The Great Ocean Road winds past a variety of good surfing locations and also passes near the Australian Surfing Museum in Torquay.

But now the Great Ocean Road zigzags its way across the landscape to its official end at Allanford, a small village outside Warrnambool. Warrnambool is a large regional centre, a veritable bustling city by the standards of the small communities which the Great Ocean Road has connected. For the tourist it offers whale-watching, and the delights of Middle

Island with its charming population of penguins guarded by sheepdogs.

The Great Ocean Road is a drive through everything that southern Australia has to offer. It is a slide show of habitats, a parade of villages and townships with their origins in the earliest European settlement of the continent. But above

all it is a constantly changing view of the seas which can wreck the best laid plans and wash away roads and cliffs; seas which mankind has tried to harness for profit, for discovery and for pleasure. Enjoy!

Grossglockner High Alpine Road

Austria

Length: 62 km, 39 miles
Start: Bruck
Finish: Heiligenblut
Highlights: Edelweissspitze, Fusch Summit, Hochtor Summit, Pasterze Glacier

On the highest ridge of mountains in the Alps sits Austria's loftiest peak, the Grossglockner, 3,798 metres (12,460 ft) above sea level. The Grossglockner High Alpine Route almost matches it for altitude as it snakes its way up and over the 2,504-metre Hochtor Pass.

A mountain pass is always an evocative route, a journey from one world to another, usually by an arduous, personally challenging path. It's a philosophical transformation as much as a road trip. So it is with the Grossglockner High Alpine Route (GHAR). It crosses the Great Alpine Divide, the watershed spine of the Alpine Region. Waters to the north of here all flow north into the Salzbach and Inn rivers which join the Danube at Passau in Germany; to the south they join the mighty Drava which drains parts of Italy, Austria, Slovenia and Hungary before joining the Danube around 1,000 km downstream from Passau on the border between Croatia and Serbia.

This is a dramatic, twisting, often steep drive, requiring plenty of concentration from your driver. Expect distracting views of waterfalls, lakes, glaciers, rocky outcrops and snow-crowned mountains.

The idea of the GHAR was derided when first proposed in 1924. The idea of tourism in which the road itself was the attraction seemed laughable when roads were uncomfortable and cars were scarce – according to some sources there were at the time as few as 150,000 vehicles in all of Austria, Germany and Italy, the target markets. The idea was revived at the height of the Great Depression as a means of relieving unemployment. There were more cars on the roads by then, but the target of attracting 120,000 visitors still seemed risible. Nevertheless the dramatic drive was officially launched in 1935 with a road race for cars and motorcycles which attracted an international field.

LEFT: The road has numbered hairpins up to the Hochtor Pass at 2,504 metres (8,215 ft).

BELOW: A snow-capped Johannisberg Mountain beyond the Wilhelm Swarovski Observatory.

By 1938 visitor numbers were 375,000, three times that first target. The original single-lane surface has been improved and considerably widened over the years and about 350,000 cars and coaches travel its 62 km each year. It's a toll road too, and in 2019 a day ticket for a car cost 36.5 euros; so who's laughing now?

The route leaves the town of Bruck heading south on Route 107, between the steep sides of the narrow Fusch valley. At Ferleiten a large car park and some toll booths mark the start of the adventure. Note that the road is liable to closure in bad weather at any time of the year, and is never open overnight. If you find the road ahead closed there is accommodation here.

The road climbs, clinging to the left-hand side of the valley before doubling back on itself repeatedly in a series of four hairpin bends to gain extra height. In the range of mountains opposite sits the Grosses Wiesbachhorn, a 3,564-metre (11,693-ft) mountain encircled by glaciers, and at Hochmais rest area you feel almost as if you are level with the peaks.

But you are not. A further set of six tortuous hairpins raises you another 300 metres (984 ft) in less than 3 km. And still you climb, past a Museum of Alpine Nature with insights into the geology and biology of this lofty environment, until a series of nine extreme bends make the final assault on Fusch Summit, the lower of two climaxes of this route. Just before you reach it, take a turning on the left. The direct route from Bruck to Heiligenblut is a mere 48 km in length, but there are two indispensable side roads from it. This, the first, takes you to Edelweissspitze, Edelweiss Point, a viewpoint of heart-in-mouth beauty across the whole of the Hohe Tauern mountain range. The air genuinely feels thinner here, but the scenery is richly, classically alpine.

Beyond Fusch Summit, at Fusch Lake, there's an exhibition about the construction of the GHAR

RIGHT: In high summer, from June 1st to August 31st, the toll road opens at 5 am and closes at 21:30.

BELOW: A traditional Austrian farm building nestled in the Salzbach Valley.

and views back across some of the hairpins that brought you to the summit. Then the road climbs, with the help of a tunnel and further hairpins, towards the border between the Austrian states of Salzburg and Carinthia. It crosses the border underground, emerging from a second tunnel at Hochtor Summit, 2,537 metres (8,323 ft). Hoch Tor means 'high gateway'. As if you needed to ask.

More hairpin bends now take you down through the upper runs of the Heiligenblut ski area. At a roundabout, you can take the second of the route's side-road detours, to Kaiser Franz Josefs Hohe, a viewpoint – unsurprisingly – made famous by the visit of Emperor Franz Josef. The 7-km road to it skirts the beautiful glacial lakes of Margaritzenstausee and Sandersee – both worth the short walk to their remote shores.

The viewpoint itself, housed now in a modern glass lantern, looks across to the Pasterze glacier and the Grossglockener mountain itself. This is as close as the route takes you to its namesake, while nearby a cable railway will lower you almost to the Pasterze valley floor, within a couple of kilometres of the glacier face. From the Emperor's Viewpoint you can retrace your route and complete the descent into Heiligenblut, a

pretty alpine resort offering canyon rafting and walking trails in the summer to complement its extensive winter sports facilities. For now though, the driver of your vehicle will be grateful, after 53 hairpin bends, for a few moments of quiet meditation on the smallness of man in the vastness of the mountains.

Guoliang Tunnel Road

Henan Province, China

Length: 55 km, 35 miles
Start: Huixian
Finish: Guoliang
Highlights: The journey

Most interesting roads have attention-grabbing alternative names. China's Guoliang tunnel has one of the most arresting: 'The Road That Does Not Tolerate Mistakes'.

The precarious route links the previously isolated village of Guoliang with the outside world. Its most famous feature is the road tunnel carved inside a cliff. Hewn from the rock high in the remote Taihang Mountains, part of China's Henan Province, the narrow tunnel is around 1.2 km long. It has 30 windows of varying shapes and sizes. As well as letting light in, they were also used to dispose of rubble from the construction process. In addition to framing the surrounding mountain scenery, they highlight the deep drop on one side of the road. This drop is not so alarming when in the tunnel but it becomes rather more worrying on one section of the road which is just an open ledge.

The story of the road's origins is as remarkable as the views. As late as the early 1970s, the only route in or out of the village was a series of 720 stone steps known as the Sky Ladder. Steep, narrow and treacherous when wet, the steps were strangling Guoliang's survival as a community. When the central authorities declined to help, the villagers decided to build their own lifeline. Armed with only the most basic of engineering knowledge, the thirteen strongest villagers started digging into the rock. Some sources state that the workers did not use any power tools, just hammers and drills – some

4,000 hammers and 12 tonnes of drill rods, according to one report. Other sources say that explosives were used. Either way, the tunnel was started in 1972 and finished five years later.

If the story is to be believed, the villagers sold vital numbers of livestock to buy tools and even neglected their crops in order to complete the road. Their gamble paid off. Deng Xiaoping opened up China to tourism in the late Seventies and Guoliang has reaped the rewards.

Location scouts for the Chinese film industry were delighted to discover the stone-built village houses which were seemingly untouched by much 20th-century progress. Domestic and foreign visitors followed along with significant investment in the area's tourism infrastructure. While Guoliang may be modernizing, the road tunnel which links it to the outside world retains its rough-hewn authenticity. Not to mention its reputation as a road which punishes mistakes.

BELOW: With the village perched on the edge of a cliff, the immense task facing the villagers was clear to see.

The Hana Highway

Hawaii, USA

Length: 51 miles, 82 km
Start: Kahului
Finish: Hana
Highlights: Baldwin Beach, Twin Falls, Waikamoi Nature Trail, Upper Waikani Falls, Pua'a Ka'a Falls, Pi'ilanihale Heiau

Someone has counted all the bends on the 50-mile route from Kahului to Hana on the Hawaiian island of Maui. There are over 600 of them, or more than twelve curves a mile.

Maui's population of around 150,000 is swollen by nearly three million visitors each year. Most who arrive at the airport of its capital town Kahului head for the west coast to soak up the sun. But a road trip along the twists and turns of the Hana Highway in the east is now firmly on the list of tourist must-do's.

It is short in distance but it shouldn't be undertaken lightly. The traffic volume is rising with its popularity; and those bends won't steer themselves. You will want to stop often, not only for the views but to prevent the onset of car-sickness. Some make a virtue of taking it slowly – there are three campsites along its route, and enough short trails and viewpoints to fill two or three days. Truly delicious fresh fruit and banana bread from roadside vendors along the way should also encourage you to stop and soak up all that Maui has to offer.

Setting off from Kahului you may wonder what all the fuss is about. It's the island's unglamorous commercial centre, not a holiday destination. The place is built on low-lying, undramatic land. The early miles are on Route 36 across a plain of farm crops and past the airport you probably just arrived at.

But these are the things you have come to Maui to leave behind, and soon you do. Shortly the road hits the coast, where Baldwin Beach Park and the smaller Ho'okipa Beach Park are both worth kicking your shoes off on. After skirting the edge of tiny Maliko Bay the road starts to climb inland, and the point at which it becomes Route 360 is the official start of the Hana Highway.

It is only 22 miles from here to Hana as the nene (the Hawaiian state bird) flies, but the winding road is 35 miles long. The engineering of this highway has presented several challenges to the

OPPOSITE: There are approximately 620 curves along Route 360 from the east of Kahului to Hana.

RIGHT: You can stop at the Surf Shop in Paia and clear your chakras with some ocean yoga.

roadbuilder. To get to Hana the route must cross the Koolau Forest Reserve. This means traversing the precarious slopes below the peaks of Pu'unianiau (6,316 ft, 1,925 metres) and Hanakauhi (7,795 ft, 2,375 metres) as they plunge to the sea. The slopes are not only steep but folded like the sides of a cloth on a circular table. Every fold has been sculpted by a tumbling mountain stream, and construction of the road required the building of 59 bridges. Starting in the 1870s it took 60 years to complete, and was only fully hard-topped in the 1960s.

It is of course precisely those forests, folds and streams, nightmares for the civil engineer, that make the Hana Highway such a paradise as a road trip. The route abounds in spectacular waterfalls, most within reach of the road by a short walk through the rainforest. The first of these is the popular Twin Falls, where a short hike through the trees is rewarded with an abundance of waterfalls and pools to swim in beneath the forest canopy.

Waikamoi Nature Trail is a well-maintained chance to glimpse a tiny corner of the nearly 9,000 acres of the Waikamoi Preserve. The area is managed by the Hawaiian Nature Conservancy to foster local flora and fauna, and there's a good chance of seeing rare plant and bird species. Watch out for the scarlet 'I'iwi bird and the patchwork bark of the Rainbow Eucalyptus, whose smooth skin is a Jackson Pollock splatter of bright shades of green and brown. The whole trail is less than two miles long. And if you like

ABOVE LEFT: An aerial view of the highway as it follows the Maui coastline.

ABOVE: The 'Seven Sacred Pools' of 'Ohe'o Gulch is not a name steeped in Polynesian history, but was given to the series of waterfalls by a local hotel trying to promote the area.

RIGHT: A spectacular grove of rainbow eucalyptus trees. They are not native to the island but were imported from the Philippines. After the bark is shed the different patches of trunk take on this staggering array of colours.

your trees, just a little further along the highway is the Garden of Eden Arboretum (admission charge) where sequences were shot for the film *Jurassic Park*.

Further still is the Ke'anae Arboretum (free). Ke'anae is a peninsula with a history. On April 1st, 1946 a tsunami destroyed the entire town of Ke'anae. Its unassuming stone church was the only building to survive. The exposed rocky shore is testament to the force of sea and wind and offers some great views of the coast and the ocean.

Back on the highway, a series of stunning waterfalls tempt you to stop and even to swim. The Upper Waikani Falls has three high waterfalls known as the Three Bears which plummet into a great swimming hole right beside the road. Pua'a Ka'a Falls, Hanawi and Makapipi are all beautiful and inviting, and the chance to experience some raging water without falling off a surfboard.

As you approach Hana, it's worth taking a short detour to Kahanu Garden. This houses a national botanical collection of plants native to the islands of Hawaii and the South Pacific, and tells the story of the cultural relationship between their peoples. But the Garden also contains Pi'ilanihale Heiau, a remarkable temple platform built of lava rock and dating back to the 14th century. It was extended in the 16th century, probably by Maui high chief Pi'ilani who, coincidentally, ordered the construction of the first road along Maui's eastern coast, now crossed by the Hana Highway. Back then, you had to cross streams not by bridges but by swinging over them on vines – a practice that used today would certainly treble your travel insurance.

Highway 12

Utah, USA

Length: 131 miles, 211 km
Start: Panguitch
Finish: Torrey
Highlights: Red Canyon, Grand Staircase-Escalante National Monument, Anasazi State Park, Boulder Mountain

Undoubtedly one of the most scenic drives in the USA, the route starts and finishes in two different national parks and is sometimes billed as 'the best of Utah in a day'.

Travelling over sandstone bluffs, spectacular forested passes and glorious colourful slick rock, Highway 12 takes you through the heart of canyon land and it's no surprise that it was designated an 'All American Road' in 2002. This is the perfect route to give you a feel for Utah and can easily be driven in an afternoon, but if you really want to enjoy it spend at least a couple of days travelling its 131 miles.

RIGHT: Morning light at Sunrise Point in Bryce Canyon National Park.

BELOW: 'White Ghosts', another name for the Wahweap Hoodoos in Grand Staircase-Escalante National Monument.

Start in Panguitch heading east and you will soon come across the startlingly beautiful Red Canyon, well deserving of its name. It is well worth taking a walk into the canyon and imagining Native Americans travelling through the vermilion-coloured rock formation, or hoodoos, that form this alien landscape. Such hoodoos can be found on every continent, but here you will find the largest concentration anywhere on earth. There are too many to count, each one a unique shape, many appearing to mimic cartoon characters or mythical beasts. Look out for a red-rock Santa Claus, complete with his sack of toys!

After the Red Canyon you reach Bryce Canyon National Park, a park worth exploring in its own right, with many geological wonders that defy description – unless you're a geologist. After passing through the town of Tropic, you will enter Grand Staircase-Escalante National Monument.

This 'staircase' traverses down 200 million years of geological history through a series of cliffs; the Pink Cliffs, the Grey Cliffs, the White Cliffs, the Vermillion Cliffs and even the Chocolate Cliffs! It was one of the last parts of the United States to be mapped, and at almost 2 million acres, it has plenty of untrammelled areas for further exploration.

As the road turns north, it rides the twists and turns of the Hogsback with steep canyons dropping sharply away on both sides. Stop in the town of Boulder to visit the remnants of a prehistoric Indian village at Anasazi State Park. Finally, you pass into the Dixie National Forest. The road follows the summit of Boulder Mountain and the trees frame the Circle Cliffs and the Henry Mountains. Travel this at sunset during fall and watch the cliffs glow with life as the golden aspen trees quake in the breeze.

TOP LEFT: Autumn snowfall in Red Canyon, part of Utah's Dixie National Forest.

TOP: A natural arch turned into a road arch in Red Canyon on Scenic Byway 12.

ABOVE: Handy for canyoneers, a ladder assists progress in Kanarra Creek, part of the Dixie National Forest.

RIGHT: There are dramatic changes of scenery; here the road sweeps through a barren, rocky section of the Grand Staircase-Escalante National Monument.

Ho Chi Minh Road

Vietnam

Length: 1,900 km, 1,180 miles
Start: Hanoi
Finish: Ho Chi Minh City
Highlights: Phong Nha, Mai Chau, Phong Nha-Ke Bang National Park, Hang Son Doong, Hue, Hoi An, Hai Van pass and tunnel

Running from Hanoi in the North of Vietnam to Ho Chi Minh City, formerly Saigon, in the South, the Ho Chi Minh Road snakes down through the west of this narrow country following the Truong Son Range or Annamese Mountains.

The recently developed Ho Chi Minh Road is not to be mistaken for the Ho Chi Minh Trail. During the Vietnam War, or, if you prefer, the American War, the Trail was a heavily bombed military supply network between North and South Vietnam. The Trail no longer exists, while the Road is one of the most scenic and enjoyable drives in South East Asia.

The mountainous nature of the road means that most commercial traffic avoids the Ho Chi Minh Road (HCMR) in favour of the straighter but much less entertaining National Route 1A, a motorway which hugs the coast. The craggy topography of the HCMR brings problems as well as benefits. In between towns, some sections of the road are as remote as they are steep.

This is especially true on the beautiful but winding western spur between Khe Sanh and Phong Nha. For many, this 230-km run is one of the most attractive stretches of the entire route

but fuel stops and food supplies are infrequent and qualified mechanics even more rare. It's not unheard of for roads to be washed out. Wise travellers plan accordingly.

From Ho Chi Minh City to Hanoi on this route is a 1,900-km trip and most leisure travellers take two to three weeks to cover the entire route. In one sense, it is a form of time travel. Hanoi and especially Ho Chi Minh City are rapidly changing, 21st-century cities with imposing skyscrapers, glitzy shopping centres and industrious manufacturing parks.

The road between the two shows a very different and almost timeless Vietnam. Limestone peaks, dense jungles, secluded waterfalls and small farming villages populate a landscape which would not have looked much different a hundred years ago. Buffalo rather than tractors still do most of the ploughing.

The majority of the route is deeply rural and while the scenes of traditional agriculture are fascinating, they can also cause the 21st-century Western urbanite to do a double take. It may be rare to see a live pig being transported on the back of a bike in Britain, Holland or Germany, but it is commonplace here.

If you want to get a feel for village life, the town of Mai Chau is on the Ho Chi Minh Road about 150 km west of Hanoi. It is a gateway to several ethnic minority villages which welcome paying overnight guests into their bamboo stilt homes.

ABOVE: To get a sense of scale for the massive Hang Son Doong, the small objects to the right of the photo are tents.

RIGHT: A river flows through the Bo Trach district of Phong Nha-Ke Bang National Park.

The surrounding villages are home to the White Thai and Muong tribes among others.

After the never-ending streams of frantic moped traffic in Hanoi, the steadier pace of life here offers some respite. Of course, while the villages are calmer than Hanoi, they are not necessarily tranquil. From cock crow onwards, there are crops to be tended, animals to be looked after and domestic tasks to be attended to.

While the HCMR gives ample opportunity to see the country's crops of rice, cassava, coffee and corn, it also passes through long stretches of uncultivated and wild countryside. Happily for those keen to take the journey at a gentle pace, the route goes through or by many stunning national parks which are studded with jungle-covered limestone karsts.

RIGHT: River boats assembled to take tourists to the Phong Nha cave which is only accessible by boat.

BELOW RIGHT: Paradise Cave was only discovered in 2005. It is a phenomenal 31 kilometres long. The initial 5 kilometres were first explored by the British Cave Research Association.

BELOW: Tourist boats on the Sông (river) Côn.

Arguably the most spectacular is the Phong Nha-Ke Bang National Park, a World Heritage Site in the Quang Binh Province near the border with Laos. The world's largest cave, Hang Son Doong, was discovered here in 2009. The dry statistics about its length, depth and width are hard to grasp so we will simply say that not only does it have its own river but it also has its own trees fed by the sunlight that filters through a huge crack in the rock. One account reckons that the cave could easily house a city block or indeed a 747 jet.

Hang Son Doong is just one of hundreds of caves which run through the Annamites. During the war, the Viet Cong used some of them as staging posts on the Ho Chi Minh Trail as well as bases which offered protection from American

bombing. As mentioned, the Trail was a network of supply routes which led from Nghe An province in the north of Vietnam down to the South of the country, with frequent incursions into Laos and Cambodia.

In parts, the HCMR is built over the old Trail. However, most of what remains of the Trail is on the Laotian side of the border and much of that has been reclaimed by the jungle. If remembering the war is an important part of your journey, the route still features significant sites from the conflict. Hamburger Hill, the scene of a bloody battle, is west of the road from A Luoi. For many, the number of lives lost in the battle for this strategically unimportant location marked a turning point in public perceptions of the war. On a more mundane level, there is

a gently crumbling US air strip by the town of Dak To. These days, farmers dry their crops on the runway where bombers once took off and landed.

A word of warning: A tragic legacy of the war is that large quantities of unexploded ordnance remain in the countryside of Vietnam, Laos and Cambodia. Leftover explosives maim and kill people to this day so think twice before heading off the more well-worn tracks in the jungle.

While venturing off the beaten track in tropical forests is not recommended, many Ho Chi Minh Road travellers deviate from the route to take in

ABOVE: A US Army lookout post from the Vietnam War overlooking the strategically important Hai Van Pass.

nearby attractions. Vietnam is a narrow country, especially at its centre, and leaving the HCMR to take in the former Imperial City of Hue or the colonial architecture of laidback Hoi An are popular detours.

Should you need any further persuasion, the latter is also renowned for the quality of both its chefs and its tailors. The chefs can knock up a delicious pork and herb-stuffed squid in about twenty minutes. The tailors will take a little longer to produce a shirt, dress or suit but then they are reputed to be the best in the country.

For drivers, the attractions of Hue and Hoi An play second fiddle to the road between them. Although the Hai Van Tunnel, opened in 2005, is the shortest route between the two cities, adventure seekers prefer to drive over the ancient Hai Van Pass. The name means 'ocean cloud pass' in reference to the sea mists that often obscure the stunning views of the coast. The pass and its hairpin bends have long been known for both their beauty and their hazards. Its fame, or infamy, was hugely boosted in 2008 when, during the *Top Gear* Vietnam special, Jeremy Clarkson referred to the pass as 'a deserted ribbon of perfection – one of the best coast roads in the world'.

Returning to the HCMR, one of the reasons for its construction was to boost tourism in remote regions where subsistence level farming was the main alternative. It has been very successful. The Ho Chi Minh Trail helped deliver military victory. The Ho Chi Minh Road is one symbol of Vietnam's continuing peace dividend.

LEFT: Looking down from the Hai Van Pass to the distant sands of Long Co beach.

TOP RIGHT: The Noon Gate (Ngo Mon) at the Imperial City in Hue.

RIGHT: One of the six elaborately decorated gates to the Imperial City. There are a further four gates to the Purple Forbidden City.

Icefields Parkway

Alberta, Canada

Length: 227 km, 143 miles
Start: Lake Louise
Finish: Jasper
Highlights: Bow Lake, Mistaya Canyon, Weeping Wall, Panther Falls, Athabasca Glacier, Glacier Skywalk, Sunwapta Falls

Originally a pack-horse route for fur trappers and First Nation peoples, the stunning Icefields Parkway now links two of Canada's finest National Parks.

Bears, caribou and mountain goats are among the more unusual hazards of the spectacular drive north-west from Lake Louise to Jasper. The road connects the Jasper and Banff National Parks and passes through the Rockies. The breathtaking scenery offers mountains capped in snow and lakes of glacial blue water, evergreen forests and the largest glacier in the Rockies.

Snowfalls are possible at any time of the year and although the road is kept open all year round, you are recommended to make the trip between May and September. At all times of year you must have a Parks permit to use the road. In winter, chains or winter tyres are a legal requirement. You should bear in mind that there is no cell phone coverage throughout the length of the Parkway, and only one gas station.

The route is at its busiest in July and August. It gets more than 200,000 vehicles in that two-month period. Most do the trip in a day, but it really is worth spending two or more on it. Book early if you want to be sure of your accommodation in the peak season.

Most people start from the southern end, near Lake Louise, a resort hamlet 60 km from Banff in Alberta. The Icefields Parkway, officially part of Highway 93, begins at the junction between the 93 and Highway 1 which leads from Lake Louise and Banff. You are already surrounded by snow-capped mountains as you set out following the Bow River upstream.

Soon you come to Herbert Lake, pretty enough; but a few kilometres further on you reach magnificent Hector Lake and Bow Lake itself, fed respectively by the Waputik and Wapta icefields high in the mountains to the west. The 93 runs along the shore of Bow Lake and you can see

LEFT: Despite the warning signs, Woodland caribou are a species at risk in Jasper National Park. There are none in Banff.

ATTENTION!

Caribou crossing next **20** km | Passage de caribous sur **20** km

at close quarters the extraordinary blue hue of meltwater from the Wapta glacier. A trail from the roadside leads to Bow Glacier Falls. Like all glaciers, Bow Glacier is retreating, but it is worth making the trek beyond the falls past Iceberg Lake to see it, providing you have the time and appropriate clothing.

After Bow Pass the road descends again, now following the short but energetic Mistaya River. The name means 'grizzly bear' in the language of the Cree nation. A stop at Mistaya Canyon, where the waters hurtle into a narrow gorge, is a must. The torrent merges with the North Saskatchewan River at the point where the Parkway bridges across the latter. Here you may refuel yourself and your vehicle at The Crossing Gas Station and Store before the road climbs again, following the North Saskatchewan and heading for Sunwapta Pass.

The river is swollen by many tributaries – Arctomys Creek, Rampart Creek, and the wide, curving arm of the Alexandra River as it rounds the northern slopes of Mount Amery. To the north of the Alexandra sits Mount Saskatchewan itself to the left and the Weeping Wall on the right – a cliff erupting with many waterfalls which freeze solid in winter.

Now the road turns left and right in a giant hairpin called the Big Bend as it gains height to reach the Pass. On the way don't miss the Panther Falls, a short walk from the road, where a jet of water spouts from a hole in a cliff. A little further on the other side of the road a trail climbs to

Parker Ridge, one of the finest viewpoints of the route, from which you can see the Saskatchewan Glacier, the longest in the Rockies.

The Saskatchewan Glacier is part of the Columbia Icefield, the largest expanse of permanent ice in the Rocky Mountains. At Sunwapta Pass there is a visitor centre, and trails lead out onto the ice of the Athabasca Glacier, another arm of the Icefield.

From the Pass, the midpoint of your journey, the Parkway begins its long descent towards Jasper. It follows the braided streams of the Sunwapta River down a narrow valley. On the way the fearless may choose to walk out onto the glass-floored Glacier Skywalk which arcs out above the valley floor with no apparent support. A similar experience may be had at the dramatic Sunwapta Falls where, just before the river joins the Athabasca River, it is funnelled into a tight gorge only a few feet wide. Viewing platforms

and a small wooden bridge take you right up to the thundering water.

Now the Icefields Parkway follows the Athabasca River to journey's end in Jasper. There is another spectacular gorge at Athabasca Falls, and the river continues to be swollen by others with their sources in the surrounding mountains – the Hooker Icefield to the southwest, and the Amethyst Lakes above Jasper itself.

This remarkable road was first built – by hand – in the 1930s, to provide relief and income during the Great Depression. The route was already popular and the road replaced an earlier Glacier Trail laid out in the 19th century for intrepid tourists drawn to the area by the new Canadian Pacific Railroad. Nowadays it attracts ever-increasing numbers of visitors ironically anxious to see a slice of Canada completely unspoilt by the hand of mankind. In that respect the Icefields Parkway does its job magnificently.

OPPOSITE LEFT: The deeply eroded Mistaya Canyon in the Banff National Park.

ABOVE LEFT: Cleared but not gritted, in winter the Icefield Parkway lives up to its name.

TOP: An old snowmobile parked outside a roadside stop near the Columbia Icefield.

ABOVE: The glacially fed Moraine Lake, 14 kilometres from Lake Louise in the Banff National Park.

Jebel Hafeet

United Arab Emirates

Length: 11 km, 7 miles
Start: Green Mubazzarah, Al Ain
Finish: Jebel Hafeet
Highlights: Green Mubazzarah park, Jebel Hafeet mountain

The road to Jebel Hafeet snakes back and forth across a rugged mountainside just because it can. It has been designed and constructed entirely for the pleasure of driving, and at speed.

The family of the Emir of Abu Dhabi has its roots in the city of Al Ain, and although his principle residence is in Abu Dhabi itself, the Emir likes to maintain a modest second palace in his ancestral home, or more precisely near the summit of Jebel Hafeet, the mountain above Al Ain.

The fun starts on the outskirts of the city at Green Mubazzarah family park, one of the oases after which the city (whose name means 'The Spring') is named. In this arid land it really is green, a large grassy landscape full of attractions including an incongruous railtrack bobsleigh and a number of hot springs.

From there, the approach to the palace and nearby hotel could have taken a relatively direct route through the rock and sand. From the intersection at Green Mubazzarah to the car park at the top it is only 6 km as the crow flies. Instead, as built by the German engineering firm of Strabag International to the Emir's specifications, the Jebel Hafeet highway takes nearly twice as long to reach its destination.

There are sixty bends, eleven of them turning through at least 180 degrees. They are perfectly engineered for camber and stability and the immaculate surface is designed to withstand the warping heat of the desert air. With an average gradient of 8 degrees, there are three lanes – two going up so that your driving pleasure won't be interrupted by getting stuck behind a slow-moving vehicle.

For those with interests beyond simply driving, Jebel Hafeet has much to offer. It boasts unique flora and fauna, much of it benefiting from the complex system of caves which run through the mountain. Marine fossils in the rock prove that the whole area was once under the sea. And after 500 early Bronze Age tombs were excavated at the base of the mountain in the 1950s, the mountain gave its name to that period of local prehistory.

Of all the attractions of Jebel Hafeet however, the road is the thing. The entire route is covered by street lighting, and driving it at night when all around is dark emphasizes the joy of driving purely for its own sake. The mountain sits on the border between Abu Dhabi and Oman and during the day the views from the top are spectacular. As you drive, be sure to set your dashcam to Record.

LEFT: Jebel Hafeet Mountain on the outskirts of Al Ain.

OPPOSITE: Like a rich man's Scalextric track, Jebel Hafeet uses every curve in the box.

London Landmarks

England

Length: 8.5 miles, 13.7 km
Start: Lambeth Pier
Finish: Tower Bridge
Highlights: Lambeth Palace, Parliament Square, Whitehall, Trafalgar Square, Admiralty Arch, The Mall, Buckingham Palace, Hyde Park Corner, National Gallery, Charing Cross Station, The Strand, Waterloo Bridge, Fleet Street, St. Paul's Cathedral, Tower of London, Tower Bridge, The Shard

This remarkable road trip threads its way through the maximum number of tourist hotspots per square mile, starts with a UNESCO World Heritage Site and ends with one, too.

Though it can be undertaken any time of the day or night (and the view towards St Paul's Cathedral from Waterloo Bridge is fantastic at night) it's best to try this one on a Sunday morning. With the roads free of traffic, your rate of progress will be determined by you and not the stop lights of the car in front.

The starting point is by Lambeth Pier, opposite Lambeth Palace which dates back to Tudor times and is the London residence of the Archbishop of Canterbury. Head straight to Lambeth Bridge, a few hundred metres away, and enjoy a sweeping view along the river of the Houses of Parliament and Big Ben/Elizabeth Tower as you cross north over the Thames. Turn right at the roundabout and within a minute you are into Parliament Square, with the UNESCO-listed Palace of Westminster looming over it in its Gothic glory.

Follow the roundabout round, taking a glance at the brooding statue of Winston Churchill, before turning left into Whitehall. Zipping along Whitehall (but observing speed limits) you pass the Cenotaph, the entrance to Downing Street, Horseguards Parade, and then your eyes will fix on the rapidly approaching Nelson's Column and Trafalgar Square.

As the hero of the Battle of Trafalgar towers above you, take a left through Admiralty Arch and you are into the Mall with the familiar regal

facade of Buckingham Palace visible between an avenue of trees. With three lanes of traffic you'll have the opportunity to dawdle towards the scene of so many Great British royal occasions.

At the Palace, take a slanting right turn up Constitution Hill, then a quick glance at the

RIGHT: Trafalgar Square. After the Mall it's straight through Admiralty Arch and take a left where that bus is.

BELOW: Parliament Square is a large roundabout and can be circled. For a microdiversion, pop a left to Westminster Abbey.

Wellington Arch as you effectively make a U-turn around the Hyde Park Corner roundabout. Then it's back down Constitution Hill, past Buckingham Palace, back down the Mall again, back through the Admiralty Arch to get a proper look at Trafalgar Square and Sir Edmund Lutyens' famous bronze lions at the base of Nelson's perch.

Keep in the left-hand lane as you cross the roundabout and take a left up towards the National Gallery past South Africa House (to your right). Before you get to the National Gallery you need to be in the right-hand lane to dive down to the right side of St Martin-in-the-Fields church with your sights firmly fixed on Charing Cross Station.

A left turn puts you onto the Strand and heading in an easterly direction towards theatreland.

There's many to choose from, not that you're stopping; the Adelphi and Vaudeville on the left, the Savoy tucked away on the right, the grand portico of the Lyceum (inevitably showing *The Lion King*) comes into view on the left as Waterloo Bridge Road joins from the right. A few more metres up the Aldwych there's the Duchess Theatre and the Novello (inevitably showing *Mamma Mia*) on the left, plus a glimpse of the historic Theatre Royal Drury Lane and finally the Aldwych Theatre.

The views from Waterloo Bridge are too good to miss so we double back round the bottom end of the Aldwych (a place usually swarming with red London buses), past Kings College and the back of Somerset House, before taking a left onto the best viewing platform of the Thames other than a riverboat cruise, Waterloo Bridge.

On the bridge look east and see the glittering spires of the City of London rising beyond the famous dome of St. Paul's, while on the Soutbank, the brutalist gem/monstrosity of the National Theatre catches the eye to the left, and to the right of the bridge is the Grade I-listed Royal Festival Hall and the Hayward Gallery. Time for another roundabout U-turn around the IMAX cinema and it's a return across Waterloo Bridge, this time with a good view of the Art Deco Savoy Hotel on the left (it's the one with the clock) and the neoclassical facade of the 1796 Somerset House to the right.

It's back round the Aldwych again, ignoring the turn into Kingsway, and on past Sir Christopher

ABOVE: Buckingham Palace, the backdrop to so many great events, such as the London Marathon and Ride London.

Wren's beautiful, under-visited church St Clement Danes, and into Fleet Street. The Royal Courts of Justice are to the left as you head towards a curious dragon sculpture on a pillar in the centre of the road. This is the ceremonial westward boundary marker for the old City of London (hence St. Martins was out in the fields), which still has some arcane rules and regulations it can bring to bear within its borders.

No time to stop at Dr. Johnson's favourite pub, the 17th-century Cheshire Cheese down an umpromising alley marked Cheshire Court on Fleet Street, as you begin to head downhill to Ludgate Circus, and St. Paul's Cathedral hoves into view. It's straight across the Faringdon Road and now the full height of Christopher Wren's more-visited London church begins to tower above you as you climb the short hill.

The road sweeps to the right, and there's a sudden lack of famous places to see (though you can make a detour left to see the Old Lady of Threadneedle Street, the Bank of England) as you pass down Canon Street, Eastcheap Street and then the grand finale, London's premier UNESCO World Heritage Site, the Tower of London. Gaze at the location of some of England's murkiest history as you pass on the north side before dropping a right and driving over another of London's much-loved landmarks, Tower Bridge. Park up and grab a break, your tour is over. Although saying that, the Shard is only two minutes away. You *should* be able to spot it…

TOP: The impressive facade of St Paul's Cathedral; not the only Christopher Wren church that is passed on this route.

RIGHT: Our route takes you to the north and east of the Tower of London.

FAR RIGHT: Tower Bridge is seldom raised these days. You'll get over.

Miami Art Deco District

Florida, USA

Length: 3 miles, 4.8 km
Start/ Finish: Art Deco Welcome Centre
Highlights: Breakwater Hotel, Marlin Hotel, Hoffman's Cafeteria Building, McAlpin Hotel, Colony Hotel, Carlyle Hotel

Miami's Art Deco district has the densest concentration of cutting edge 1930s and 1940s architecture in the world, from Art Deco to Streamline Moderne. The city has some 800 examples of the genre, and without going more than one street back from Miami Beach you can drive past some of the very best of them.

Art Deco perfectly suited Miami's wealthy pleasure-seeking visitors. It was very fashionable, very modern. Long vertical lines, rounded corners and repeated details all gave the impression of speed. Flashes of brilliant colour on otherwise white buildings reflected the jazz music of the time and suited the seaside location.

A short urban drive on Ocean Drive and Collins Avenue takes in a good dozen of the buildings which are regularly judged the finest. Start at the Art Deco Welcome Centre (1001 Ocean Drive) which shares a beautiful building with the Beach Patrol Headquarters. It's home to the Miami Design Preservation League, which first promoted awareness of the heritage value of Miami's Art Deco wealth.

Head south on Ocean Drive along the edge of palm-studded Lummus Park, with the sea to your left and a glorious parade of Art Deco on your right. On the corner of 10th Street stands the Breakwater Hotel (940 Ocean), a towering masterpiece designed by one of the three great architects of Miami, Anton Skislewicz.

ABOVE: The Breakwater Hotel, opened in 1936.

RIGHT: The seaward facade of the Beach Patrol Headquarters, designed by Robert Taylor and completed in 1934.

ABOVE: Many of the old hotels like to park a vintage car out front. This is the Park Central Hotel, built in 1937.

TOP RIGHT: Prolific Art Deco architect Henry Hohauser designed the Essex House Hotel (1938).

ABOVE RIGHT: This Streamline Moderne beauty started life as Hoffman's Cafeteria in 1940; today it's a branch of Señor Frog's.

At 7th, Park Central Hotel (640 Ocean) by another of the triumvirate, Henry Hohauser, is a good illustration of the Art Deco movement's love of symmetry and threes – three hexagonal portholes over the entrance, three balanced elements to the facade.

After First Street, turn right at traffic lights onto South Pointe Drive then right again at the next lights onto Collins Avenue. Look out at 8th Street for a spire with TIFFANY spelt out vertically in lights. That's the former name of a hotel now simply called The Hotel (801 Collins), designed by L. Murray Dixon, the third of the architects who made Miami an Art Deco paradise.

Now the Art Deco classics come thick and fast: Hohauser's Essex House Hotel (1001 Collins, on

the corner of 10th); Dixon's Marlin Hotel (1200 Collins at 12th); and two doors further, The Webster by Hohauser (1220 Collins). After 14th Street, on the corner of Collins and Española Way, is another Hohauser gem. Originally Hoffman's Cafeteria Building (1450 Collins), it has been a dancehall, gay bar and deli, and is now a branch of the Señor Frog's franchise. Its appearance is timeless.

Turn right again onto 15th Street, and first right after that to take you back onto Ocean Drive. At 1424 Ocean stands L. Murray Dixon's McAlpin Hotel. Its white frontage with strong ice-green vertical lines and equally strong terracotta horizontals is brilliant. A string of such stylish hotels lines this street – the Cavalier, the Carlyle, the Clevelander – before you return to your starting point, the Art Deco Welcome Centre and Gift Shop.

ABOVE: The exclusive Marlin Hotel (1939) has an in-house recording studio and is patronized by the likes of Jay-Z and Kanye West.

TOP RIGHT: The Colony Hotel at 763 Ocean Drive was built in 1935, along with a Colony Theatre at 1040 Lincoln Road.

RIGHT: The Carlyle Hotel (1939).

Moab Trails: Dead Horse Point Scenic Drive

Utah, USA

Length: 33 miles, 53.5 km
Start: Moab
Finish: Dead Horse Point
Highlights: Seven-mile Canyon, the Needles, the Colorado River

The view from Dead Horse Point is arguably the most spectacular vista in a land of spectacular vistas; it is claimed to be one of the most photographed viewpoints in the world, and for good reason. It is truly jaw-dropping.

Head north on US-191 from Moab before turning left on SR-313. This is not a long drive, at just 33 miles, so do take plenty of time to pull off the road for displays with excellent explanations of the geology, archaeology and scenery of these sandstone canyons and sagebrush-covered hills. You can catch views of the appropriately named Seven-mile Canyon, the Needles, and Maze. After about 14 miles turn left at the fork towards Dead Horse Point.

Dead Horse Point is a peninsula of rock perched on top of vertiginous sandstone cliffs with a narrow 25-meter (82-ft) neck of rock connecting it to the rest of the mesa. The name apparently comes from the cowboy practice of herding wild mustangs onto the point and stacking brushwood across the 'neck' to stop the horses escaping. Tragically, the cowboys sometimes left without releasing the horses, leaving them all to die of thirst with the sparkling Colorado River in plain sight. When you see the River snaking its way through the canyons over 600 heart-stopping metres (2,000 ft) below, you can imagine the hardships of those ranch hands working these harsh lands.

The Point is surrounded by the 5,362-acre Dead Horse Point State Park. It's an immense vastness of ragged red-rock canyons and towering mesas with the snow-capped La Sal and Abajo

RIGHT: The spectacular view from Dead Horse Point. Below, the Colorado River makes a stately turn.

mountains in the far distance. The nearer view is dominated by Monument Basin and a tall spire called the Totem Pole rising 93 metres (305 ft).

At this point you are 1,830 metres (6,000 ft) above sea level and you may get the urge to grab hold of something for balance. Steady your nerves, take one more look at the awe-inspiring view and then grab a coffee at the Pony Espresso coffee shop while you spare a thought for those poor horses.

ABOVE: A winter view from Dead Horse Point is equally dramatic.

OPPOSITE AND RIGHT: Another epic trail can be viewed below Dead Horse Point. Parts of the Shafer Canyon Trail were built as an access road for the potash mine that you will pass before starting the true Canyon drive. It's advisable to take nerves of steel and a suitable 4x4 vehicle for this particular trail. After 8 miles you enter the section of Canyonlands National Park known as Islands in the Sky. The famous scene in the film *Thelma and Louise*, when they drive their car off the edge and into the canyon, was filmed at this point.

Moab Trails: La Sal Mountain Loop

Utah, USA

Length: 70 miles, 113 km
Start/Finish: Moab
Highlights: 'The Priest', 'The Nuns', Castle Rock,
La Sal Mountain Pass, Lake Warner

This drive is closed through much of the winter months but during the summer it provides cool relief from the heat of the desert floor. Escape the dusty desert into the cool green alpine forests of the La Sal range.

This 70-mile, half-day drive takes you through a rainbow of scenery as you leave the red canyons for the lush green forests and colourful alpine meadows. Heading north on Highway 191, turn right onto Scenic Byway 128 just before the bridge. Soon after passing the small town of Castle Valley there appears the dramatic rock formation of The Priest soon followed by The Nuns, and Castle Rock towering above. The La Sal Mountain Loop Road turnoff is 11 miles from Scenic Byway 128.

Slowly the small pinyon pines and juniper trees give way to oaks, large pines and aspen groves as you continue on your drive up over La Sal Mountain Pass, one of the highest in Utah. If you are feeling energetic you can stop to hike the tallest mountain in the state, Mt. Peale. In contrast to the silent desert below, this is a noisy place. Pines whisper; aspens quake; brooks babble.

As you come down from the pass, watch out for a glimpse of a beautiful mountain lake surrounded by white-barked aspen trees which frame the mountains in the background. Turn down the dirt road to reach it. This is Warner Lake, a great place to spend a night if you are camping – you will need to reserve a pitch via the government website.

The view from the lakeshore makes for a stunning picture, especially in the autumn when the yellows of the aspen leaves reflect in the still surface of the lake and the snow-capped mountains dominate the skyline. Breathe. All around you are wildflower meadows and the buzz of insects collecting nectar and you will feel like the heat of the desert is a lifetime away. And no one will stop you if you want to brave a cold plunge in the icy water.

RIGHT: The mountain road from Castle Valley in the Manti-La Sal National Forest, which covers more than 1.2 million acres (4,900 square kilometres).

BELOW: Aspens provide autumn colour in the Manti-La Sal National Forest.

Monument Valley

Arizona, USA

Length: 17 miles, 27.4 km
Start/Finish: Oljato-Monument Valley
Highlights: A monumental photo opportunity

An ancient valley of towering red-rock pinnacles, isolated buttes, colossal mesas and wide open spaces, Monument Valley is one of the USA's iconic landscapes, little changed in 3000 years.

For a truly breathtaking drive, take a sunrise tour and watch the dawn light breathe life into this spectacular landscape. Monument Valley is a place to visit for quiet contemplation of what nature can create with nothing but wind, water, sand and time. Visit at any time of year, but light snow during the winter months will produce an unforgettable landscape of intense contrasts and beautiful imagery.

The main drive through this Jurassic landscape is a 17-mile circular drive passing many of the most popular sites in Monument Valley. This is on dirt roads, but a 4x4 is not a necessity; the road is just bumpy and dusty! If you are nervous of taking your hire car on dirt roads, hire a Navajo guide who will take you round in their own vehicle. And while the main loop is the only one you can self-drive, it is worth paying for a tour to

take you to some of the less popular but equally spectacular parts of the valley, and give you the opportunity to see petroglyphs and Anasazi sites. Since the valley forms part of the Navajo Nation Reservation, a Navajo guide will also be able to provide insights on the landscape and wildlife that you could never hope to achieve on your own, as well as a window into the culture of the people that still call this landscape home.

RIGHT: The Navajo were driven from this land by Colonel Kit Carson in the 1860s, but were allowed to return when no great precious metal ore was found. Today there is tourist gold in them there hills.

Monument Valley can be a busy place to visit, especially during the peak holiday times. So, if you are in search of real solitude and are looking to spend it in a setting almost as spectacular, it is worth travelling on a few miles to the northeast along US-163, to find the Valley of the Gods. This is Monument Valley's little-explored sister and, if you stay into the evening on a moonless night, you will think the heavens are exploding with the number of stars.

RIGHT: Ancient Anasazi petroglyphs carved on a sandstone butte in Monument Valley.

FAR RIGHT: The 'Ear of the Wind' natural arch in Monument Valley. There is a similar arch named 'Eye of the Sun'.

BELOW: View of Monument Valley looking south on US-163.

OPPOSITE: More classic western sandstone in the Valley of the Gods, part of the Bears Ears National Park.

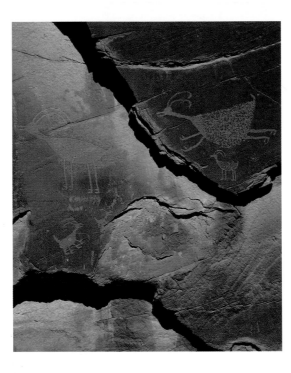

North Coast 500

Scotland

Length: 500 miles, 800 km
Start/Finish: Inverness Castle
Highlights: Bealach na Ba, Poolewe, Corrieshalloch Gorge, Ullapool, Ardvreck Castle, Lochinver, Inverpolly, Smoo Cave, Dornoch

The North Coast 500 is not a road trip for a driver unsure about the width of their vehicle or reversing. It follows the rugged coast of northern Scotland on roads which are often little wider than a single vehicle, with small fishing villages and ruined castles dotting the mountainous landscape along the route.

Scotland has long been a popular destination for holidaymakers. Inevitably the most accessible sites are the ones most visited by tourists – the capital city Edinburgh and its world-renowned festival, historic Stirling and the grandeur of Loch Lomond for example. Intrepid travellers might get as far as the Isle of Skye and Loch Ness.

Because of its great distance from Scotland's principal cities of Glasgow and Edinburgh, the far north of the country has remained largely undiscovered. In 2015 however, the North Coast 500 or NC500 was devised, a route which on a map literally outlined this forgotten area, giving it a shape and an identity in the hope of boosting visitor numbers. It has succeeded beyond all expectations.

The NC500 begins in Inverness, the regional capital and a vital commercial centre serving the surrounding rural communities. From its starting point below the city's 19th-century castle, the NC500 heads west, passing the spectacular Rogie waterfall and eventually following the railway tracks of the Kyle Line as they thread their way through highland glens to the sea at Lochcarron, now a quiet backwater but a natural deepwater harbour once used for the construction of oil rigs.

A few miles beyond Lochcarron the road climbs away through a narrow pass where you need to use the designated 'passing places' to allow overtaking and to meet oncoming vehicles. This is Bealach na Ba, the Pass of the Cattle, through which the road reaches remote Applecross village. The pass got its name from cattle trading, but these days you are more likely to see wild deer on the tarmac.

The Bealach road clings to a steep hillside or twists in impossible hairpin bends, rising from sea level to cross the 600-metre (1,968-ft) high pass. Applecross lies at sea level on the other side, a vibrant community which until the construction of the Bealach road in the early 20th century was only accessible by sea.

A second road to Applecross was engineered later in the century and it is this road which the NC500 now follows around the coast to the sealochs of Shieldaig and Torridon. This is an ancient landscape, formed by a sequence of events which geologists now call Torridonian.

As the NC500 heads north, the Torridonian mountains assume extraordinary shapes, the result of 750 million years of erosion. These are some of the oldest rocks in Britain.

Beyond Torridon the road follows majestic Loch Maree to the harbour town of Gairloch, and to Poolewe where the influence of the warm Gulf Stream makes the lush gardens of Inverewe House possible at such a northerly latitude.

Soon the road turns inland and climbs steadily to Corrieshalloch Gorge, 60 metres (197 ft) deep and a mile long, carved by the waters of the Droma during the last ice age. Now, on a footbridge and viewing platform, you can stand over the gorge watching the 45-metre (148-ft) high Falls of Measach tumble into it, before you follow the stream down to the sea again at Ullapool. Ullapool is the largest village on this north-western coast, a ferry port serving

the Outer Hebrides and home to the last major supermarket on the NC500 for 165 miles. North of Ullapool the road enters Inverpolly Nature Reserve and the Northwest Highlands Geopark, a UNESCO-designated area of outstanding geology and geography. This corner of the world is Britain's last true wilderness, a land of eagles and stags. Here, old Torridonian Sandstone rests on ancient Lewisian Gneiss laid down 2,600 million years ago.

Human intervention in the landscape is sporadic. Set back from Loch Assynt are the Bone Caves of Inchnadamph where the bones of bears and wolves long absent from Scotland have been found. On the shores of the loch stands Ardvreck Castle, ruined stronghold of the ruthless Macleod clan. Everywhere, ruined stone cottages are evidence of the cruel practice of the Highland Clearances, in which rich 18th- and 19th-century landowners simply cleared the native inhabitants from the land to make way for more profitable sheep. The story of a remarkable

reclaiming of the land is told, alongside others, in Lochinver Tourist Centre.

Leaving Lochinver the NC500 follows the coast past isolated beaches at Clachtoll and Clashnessie, almost encircling the mountainous ramparts of Quinag before a graceful modern bridge carries travellers across the narrow stretch of sea at Kylesku. That crossing, made by ferry until 1984, takes you into another world even emptier and more desolate than the last, a waterworld of peat bogs, lochs and streams. Crossing the rivers of Laxford and Rhiconich you eventually follow the River Dionard on its long slow descent to Durness, the most northwesterly settlement on the British mainland, beloved of John Lennon who spent holidays there as a child.

A mile after the road turns eastwards lies Smoo Cave, a cave system scoured out both by freshwater stream and by the action of the sea pounding into a saltwater gorge at the cave's mouth. The sea off this north coast of Scotland

is one of the most dangerous stretches of Britain's waters, with ferocious currents even at slack tide on a calm day. There are relatively few settlements along the road as it winds its way across moors and around deep inlets before arriving in Thurso, the second largest town on the NC500. Vehicle ferries depart from nearby Scrabster and Gill Bay to the Orkney islands.

TOP: Scourie on the west coast. A cheerful signpost on the A894 directs traffic to 'The Beach and Burial Ground'.

ABOVE: Ullapool on Loch Broom on the west coast. You can catch a ferry to Stornoway in the Hebrides if you change your mind about the North Coast 500.

A passenger ferry also runs to Orkney from John O'Groats, famous for being one end of the longest possible journey on the British mainland – Land's End in Cornwall being the other. From this north-eastern extremity the NC500 now turns southwards.

This eastern coast differs in character from both the northern and the western legs of this road trip. There are few beaches but few inlets too, in contrast to the fjord-like west coast. A railway line between Inverness and Thurso and Wick opened in 1874 bringing prosperity in the form of trading opportunities and visitors. The fishing villages are more prosperous, the farms generally on better land here than the poor terrain of the north.

The east coast shows signs of Scotland's early inhabitants too. The Picts, with no written language, left their mark on finely decorated standing stones from the 5th to the 8th centuries, examples of which have been found all along this shore.

The Picts were displaced by invading Vikings, whose placenames survive as evidence of their presence – Wick, for example, is the Norse word for a village; and 'dale', as in Berriedale and Helmsdale, is the Scandinavian word for a valley, used along this coast in preference to the Gaelic word 'glen'. Sutherland, the name of the county through which much of the NC500 runs, is also Viking in origin – it may be the northern tip of the Scottish mainland, but seen from Orkney – which was then ruled by Norway – it was paradoxically the 'southern land'.

Sutherland saw some of the worst examples of the Highland Clearances, and the 2nd Duke of Sutherland built his stately home Dunrobin Castle with the profits from the practice from 1835 onwards. The Castle, between Brora and Golspie, is now open to the public, but remains the Sutherland family seat.

The administrative seat of Sutherland is the handsome town of Dornoch which boasts fine beaches and golf. From here on, passing through the towns of Dingwall and Beauly, the population increases noticeably as the NC500 nears its end back at Inverness Castle.

The North Coast 500 has already won a place on lists of routes to travel. The scenery is breathtaking and the diversity of human impact (or absence) on it fascinating. Its overwhelming success has put a strain on local resources, particularly of accommodation. You are strongly advised to plan ahead, and to consider camping as an option. Bear in mind that phone and data coverage is patchy in such empty country. The roads are slow up there, narrow and winding; and the journey will be slower and better the more often you get out of your car.

OPPOSITE: The entrance to Smoo Cave near Durness. Local guides advise that even a small amount of rain can cause the cave to flood.

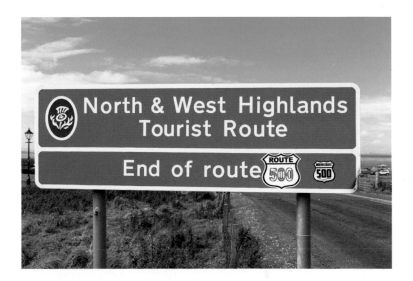

Nürburgring Nordschleife

Germany

Length: 21 km, 13 miles
Highlights: Blind corners, motor racing history

With a similar vintage to the Monaco GP circuit, there is no more historic race track existing in its original format than the exhilarating Nürburgring Nordschleife.

Numerous blind corners, heart-in-mouth crests and a variety of road quality along its 20.832 km length all make the Nordschleife challenging for even the most skilled, professional drivers. The testing route and dark, forest location in the Eifel mountains led to it being labelled the Green Hell by Sir Jackie Stewart. And that was after he won the 1968 Grand Prix there. The Austrian Formula One driver Jochen Rindt reckoned it was 'difficult to drive, easy to die' on the track.

It certainly has a deadly history. The first racing driver fatality occurred there in 1928, less than a year after it opened. Niki Lauda suffered terrible burns when he crashed his car there during the 1976 German Grand Prix. The incident led to the Nordschleife being dropped as a stop on the Grand Prix tour. A brand new grand prix track was built just to the south of the old road and completed in 1984. While the new track boasts all the latest safety features, the original continues to exert a powerful allure. It is very popular with car manufacturers as a test track for their latest models.

The producers of *Top Gear* certainly recognize its appeal to petrolheads; the track has been used as a location many times by the show. Nordschleife is regularly open to the public

and, for a fee, civilians in their own vehicles can follow in the tyre tracks of racing legends. When planning such a trip, it is best to check that your insurance will cover any accidents. Many insurers exclude Nordschleife from their cover. A safer but possibly more hair-raising option is to hitch a paid ride with a professional racing driver. Unless your driving skills happen to be on a par with those of Lewis Hamilton, you are unlikely to experience quite such a short ride if you drive yourself. However, Nordschleife's genuinely iconic status means that those of us with petrol in our veins can enjoy its charms at less life-threatening speeds.

ABOVE: The famous Carousel (Karussell) banked, 180-degree corner, photographed during the 1972 German Grand Prix. Formula 1 cars would regularly get airborne at this circuit.

LEFT: Adenauer Police report that in 2017 there were 81 accidents on the circuit, two fatalities, 18 serious injuries and 43 minor injuries, mostly from drivers overestimating the speed which they could carry through the corners.

The Overseas Highway

Florida, USA

Length: 113 miles, 182 km
Start: Miami
Finish: Key West
Highlights: Key Largo, Marathon, Bahia Honda State Park, Big Pine Key, Key West

The Overseas Highway threads the jewels of the Florida Keys like a necklace. Some sixty-seven small islands perched on a graceful arc of coral reefs form the border between the Gulf of Mexico and the Atlantic Ocean, stretching more than 100 miles out to sea from mainland Florida.

Florida was given its name by Juan Ponce de Leon, a companion of Christopher Columbus and the first European to map the area. His attempts to settle the land were strongly resisted by the native tribes, whose word for an island was *cairi*. This became 'cay' in Spanish and 'key' in English.

In the days when it was safer to travel by sea than by land, the Florida Keys were well placed intermediaries for trade between South America, the West Indies and North America. They also profited from the numerous shipwrecks in the area. Over time, as their fortunes declined, the Keys remained accessible only by boat at the start of the 20th century.

All that changed thanks to one Henry Flagler, known as the Father of Miami, who owned a chain of hotels along Florida's east coast. He built a railroad connecting them all; and when plans for the Panama Canal were announced, he saw an opportunity to capture shipping trade if he could extend his line to Key West, the outermost cay, which is blessed with a deep natural harbour.

Flagler's trains reached Key West in 1912. The cost of the extension, some $50 million, was a heavy burden of debt for the railroad company to bear. When the Storm of the Century struck the Keys in 1935 and washed nearly half the track into the sea, the bankrupt Florida East Coast Railroad Company could not afford to rebuild. Plans were already being considered for a road transport link through the Keys, and these plans now simply incorporated the bridges and causeways recently vacated by the railroad. The complete Overseas Highway was opened in 1938.

Heading south from Miami, US Highway 1 runs down the eastern edge of the Everglades

RIGHT: The Mile 0 sign on US 1 at Key West.

OPPOSITE: Pigeon Key on Seven Mile Bridge. The Florida Keys Heritage Trail is to the right.

National Park, before making its way onto Key Largo. At 33 miles this is the longest of the Keys and the starting point of the Florida Keys Overseas Heritage Trail, a traffic-free route to Key West for cyclists and walkers. The Florida Keys reef is the only living coral reef in the continental USA, and Key Largo is a good place from which to explore it above or below the water. Beyond Key Largo, on Islamorada, there's a Museum of the History of Diving.

The islands are divided into Upper, Middle and Lower Keys; Long Key is the last of the Uppers and a long bridge from there takes you to the Middles, which are occupied by the city of Marathon. This is a popular fishing centre and a good place to stop for seafood. It also hosts the Dolphin Research Centre and a hospital for injured sea turtles.

At the south-western end of Marathon the impressive Seven Mile Bridge carries you over the waves to the Lower Keys, with a good view of the old railroad bridge beside it. The bridge

touches down at the almost uninhabited Bahia Honda Key. The island is a state park where you can find a remarkable range of rare insects, birds, plants and fish. Its beach was voted America's finest in 1992, and the channel beside it is one of the deepest through the Keys – part of the old railroad bridge has been removed to allow the passage of sailing vessels through it. Bahia Honda means 'deep bay'.

From Bahia Honda the Highway proceeds to Big Pine Key, one of the largest islands in the chain. Before the arrival of the railroad and then highway it used to be a ferry port. It is home to a population of the endangered Key deer, a species which lives in the Lower Keys and nowhere else. In the 1950s there were only around twenty-five Key deer left. Now they number around 800 in total, but road kill by drivers on the Overseas Highway accounts for as many as 150 deaths a year.

From here on, the Overseas Highway seems to cross more ocean than land, in a combination of causeways and bridges which barely touch down on the many small Keys between Big Pine and its destination, Key West. Boca Chica Key, 'little mouth island', is now home to the three runways of the Key West Naval Air Station, the largest in Florida.

The International Airport of Key West is just a few miles further on. Key West is the largest of the towns on the Keys and in the 19th century it was the largest in Florida, thanks to its fishing and salvage industries. It remained a Union naval base when the rest of Florida joined the Confederacy during the Civil War; and its proximity to Cuba, only 90 miles away, has placed it at the centre of tensions between Cuba and the US. The Pan American (Pan Am) airline was founded in Key West, originally to deliver mail and passengers to and from Havana.

Each of the Florida Keys has its own story to tell. There is much to discover of American history, geography, botany and zoology; and the road is one of only thirty or so to be designated an All-American Highway.

OPPOSITE: The old Bahia Honda Rail Bridge which was originally part of the Overseas Railway built in 1912 by Florida developer Henry Flagler.

RIGHT: Mostly seen on Big Pine Key, the key deer is the smallest North American deer species and only found in Florida.

BELOW: Definitively the end of your progress on land.

Pacific Coast Highway

California, USA

Length: 860 miles, 1,384 km
Start: California/Oregon border
Finish: Dana Point
Highlights: Pelican Bay, Humboldt Redwoods Park, Trinidad Head, Sea Ranch Chapel, Golden Gate Bridge, Santa Cruz Boardwalk, the Big Sur, Bixby Creek Bridge, Venice Beach

The California coast has something for everyone, with remote beaches and redwood forests in the north and the highly developed seaside leisure activities of the south. Start your journey in the north, and you will always be on the seaward side of the road, as close to the beaches and cliffs of the Pacific Ocean as possible.

The first place you come to, as you cross the California state line from Oregon on Route 101, is Pelican Bay. Here rocky offshore islets protect a long sandy shore and – if you're lucky – yours will be the only footprints on it.

Crescent City, the most northerly centre of population on this coast, is named for its arc-shaped beach. South of here, at Gold Bluff, the sands are just as beautiful but the rip currents and heavy swell are dangerous. Surfers are replaced by wandering elk; offshore lies Reading Rock Marine Reserve, and behind you rise the pine forests of Prairie Creek Redwood Park. This section of Route 101 is known as the Redwood Highway and further south you can drive the 31-mile-long Avenue of Giants which runs parallel to the main road through Humboldt Redwoods Park.

The route runs inland to these redwoods, but where it meets the sea it is in small fishing communities like Trinidad. The lighthouse on the cliff of Trinidad Head does what it can to warn shipping of the forest of seastacks around it, but it can do nothing for the tsunamis which have regularly struck the town's harbour following seismic events elsewhere.

From Leggett the road winds down to the sea again through woodland, now following Route 1. Between Rockport and Port Arena it is called the Shoreline Highway and the road is often only a few feet from the pounding waves. It passes through the US Army's Fort Bragg, the largest military base in the world. Nearby, in contrast, the Mendocino Botanical Gardens sit on cliffs where the sea air is particularly favourable for growing rhododendrons. Further south, Point Arena has a reputation as a northern outpost of San Francisco's hippy culture; and it is home to another endangered species, the Point Arena mountain beaver.

If the magnificent ocean in all its moods is not enough to lift your spirits, watch out for the extraordinary organic form of the tiny roadside Sea Ranch Chapel, designed by architect James Hubbell in 1985. Beyond here the road continues to hug the shore as far as long, narrow Tomales Bay, which lies on the San Andreas Fault. From there the route skirts the Marin Hills before making its final approach through Sausalito to enter San Francisco across the iconic Golden Gate Bridge.

San Francisco needs no introduction, familiar around the world in thousands of movie scenes. Its hills, its cable cars, its counter-culture and its early history all deserve a fair measure of your time. It's a city that gets under your skin and it marks a step-change in this road trip. From here onwards the Pacific Coast is an altogether more populated place, and its use changes too – behind you, its advantages as a resource for making a living; ahead, its potential for leisure activities. To the north, fishing; to the south, surfing. Same great coast however.

At Santa Cruz, for example, the Boardwalk is a hedonistic heaven of pleasure rides alongside a beach devoted to windsurfing and paddle-boarding. Colourful Monterey is famous for its music – the long-running Jazz Festival was first staged in 1958, and in 1967 performances by Jimi Hendrix, Janis Joplin, Otis Redding and

OPPOSITE: Battery Point Lighthouse near Crescent City on the Redwood Coast.

BELOW: A fogbound fishing fleet docked at Crescent City.

the Who at the Monterey Pop Festival defined the hippies' Summer of Love. The city has been immortalized in novels by former resident Armistead Maupin. Neighbouring Carmel-by-the-Sea is renowned for its artistic community and its coastal beauty.

It's not all man-made pleasure however. From Carmel for a hundred miles, Route 1 rides the most famous stretch of the entire Pacific coast of America, the Big Sur. Alternating between high cliffs and low beaches this is a breathtaking few hours of driving which sticks close to the sea. Castle Rock gives you the perfect photograph of the route with beach, cliffs and the celebrated Bixby Creek Bridge. Point Piedras Blancas with its historic lighthouse juts out into the ocean and offers further spectacular views of the Big Sur both north and south.

After Lompoc, Route 1 rejoins Route 101. Santa Barbara is the setting for the best example of California's twenty-one historic Spanish missions. South-east of there, at Oxnard, you can take a trip out to the Channel Islands archipelago – a chance to travel across the Pacific Ocean at last

LEFT: A treehugger's delight, the Avenue of the Giants in the Humboldt Redwoods State Park.

BELOW: Very California; the non-denominational Sea Ranch Chapel, part of the low-impact Sea Ranch Community in Sonoma County.

instead of just alongside it. Most of the islands are a protected national park, housing many species found nowhere else in the world.

And finally, the Pacific Coast Highway arrives in Los Angeles – more familiar to us all even than San Francisco thanks to the presence of the Hollywood film and television industry in the north of the city. At the coast, the surfers on Malibu Beach are followed by the pleasure-seekers on the rides at Santa Monica Pier, and the body-builders, street artists and other exhibitionists of Venice Beach.

In fact a whole string of beaches – Long Beach, Newport, Laguna – now accompanies you to journey's end at Dana Point, where a rocky promontory is pierced by three sea arches. If you swam in the sea earlier along the route, do it again now – you'll appreciate the warmer water 860 miles further south. If you haven't swum yet, you've no excuse. It's time to get out of your car.

ABOVE: The classic Pacific Coast Highway photo, a view of the 1932 Bixby Bridge, south of San Francisco.

RIGHT: The marina at Dana Point in Orange County, the official end of the PCH.

Paris by Night

France

Length: 19km, 11.7 miles
Start/Finish: Place de la Concorde
Luxor Monument, Champs-Élysées, Arc de
Triomphe, Grand Palais, Hôtel des Invalides, Champ
de Mars, Eiffel Tower, Trocadéro, Pont l'Alma, Notre-
Dame Cathedral, Pont Neuf, Louvre Pyramid, Palais
Garnier, Place Vendôme

**Some cities look great at night, but only Paris
looks *sensationelle*...**

In daylight hours *les rues et les quais de* Paris
are populated by drivers keen to get to their
destination quickly and circling the broad,
cobbled roundabout of the Arc de Triomphe
is not for the fainthearted – eyes must be kept
firmly on the road (preferably by both occupants
of the front seats).

However, once the commuting rush is over by
9pm, the wide streets are a far less intimidating
place – the capital city of romance is a more
attractive prospect when there are fewer drivers
on the road. To add to the atmosphere, all the
major landmarks are illuminated until 1am in the
morning and motorists can take what is an utterly
enchanting city drive.

Unlike our London trip, this is a circular route. We
start in the largest square in the French capital,
the Place de la Concorde. After circulating around
the Luxor Monument, exit towards the Arc de
Triomphe along the Champs-Élysées (selecting
the tune of the same name for the car stereo).

Like riders in the Tour de France on the final
stage of the race, you circle round the colossal

Arc and head back down the Champs-Élysées
for three-quarters of its length. Then make a
right turn into Avenue Winston Churchill, passing
between the Grand Palais and the Petit Palais.

We catch our first glimpse of the River Seine
as we cross straight over the Pont Alexandre III,
driving across the Quai D'Orsay into the Parc des
Invalides, heading towards the imposing Hôtel

OPPOSITE: The Eiffel Tower photographed from the Trocadéro,
across the river Seine.

RIGHT: A rare sight of the Arc de Triomphe without traffic.

BELOW: Looking from the Quai de Gesvres towards the Pont
Notre-Dame and the Conciergerie on the Île de la Cité.

The Avenue Joseph Bouvard will take you right across the Champ de Mars, the large open space which lies in the shadow of the tower and stretches all the way from the river to the École Militaire. To get a more sustained look at the Eiffel Tower, there's a chance to circle round the Bassins du Champ de Mars halfway across and then head back to Avenue de Suffren, where a right turn will have you heading for the river again.

When you reach the Seine, it's a right turn onto the Quai Branly, sparing a few moments to appreciate the magnifique Trocadéro across the river from the Eiffel Tower. Now you are in for a long drive along the Quai, which becomes the Quai d'Orsay at the famous Pont de l'Alma. This is the bridge with the famous Zouave statue (there used to be more than one) against whom the water level is assessed when the Seine threatens to flood Paris.

Follow the Quai down to the Pont de la Concorde, then it's a left turn across the bridge, and a quick right to follow the river on the other side. We pass along the Quai des Tuileries which changes name to Quai François Mitterand, Quai de la Mégisserie and then Quai des Gesvres in quick succession as we head east towards the Île de la Cité. Take the third bridge onto the island, the Pont de Notre-Dame, which becomes the Rue de la Cité once on the isle, and after a few hundred metres on your left is that great cathedral beloved of hunchbacks.

Take a left turn and you can swing round onto the Rue du Cloître-Notre-Dame and pass by the length of the great building on the north side. At the far end it's a left onto the Quai aux Fleurs, which becomes Quai de la Corse then Quai de l'Horloge as you drive all the way around the northern edge of the Île. Then it's left across the Pont Neuf (the 'new bridge' is the oldest bridge in Paris, started in 1578) and take a right onto the Quai de Conti. Pass by the Pont des Arts

TOP: The Pont de l'Archevêché leading to Notre-Dame Cathedral on the Île de la Cité .

ABOVE: Pont Neuf (New Bridge) is the oldest in Paris.

des Invalides. Take a slanting right onto Avenue de la Motte-Picquet which takes you past the front of the grand École Militaire. Glance to your right and you'll see a familiar sight. You are approaching the iconic symbol of Paris, the Eiffel Tower. Once the military academy ends, take a right onto Avenue Suffren. Follow this for about 500 metres before taking what will be your fourth turn on the right.

footbridge, before taking the next road bridge back across the Seine, the Pont du Carrousel.

Now you should be facing the Louvre complex and providing the gate in the arch is open you can drive through into the Place du Carrousel with the great glass Pyramid du Louvre to your right. As you head out the other side, onto the great shopping street Rue de Rivoli, you cannot go straight on, so you need to take a left into Rue de Rivoli and then a swift right into Rue de l'Échelle before turning left onto the Avenue de l'Opéra.

The road passes to the right of the grand building, home of the Opéra National de Paris, and there is a roundabout in the Place Diaghilev behind, which will allow you to drive back round on the other side of the opera house and join briefly the Rue Auber. We're close to completing our circuit now and it's straight on across the Boulevard des Capucines into the Rue de la Paix, leading into the upmarket surroundings of the Place Vendôme, with its famous column.

Keep going, or take a circuit to admire the upscale shops and the Ritz Hotel, before heading south into the Rue de Castiglioni, which takes you to the Rue de Rivoli. One final turn *a droit* and you are heading towards Place de la Concorde ready to do it all *encore un fois*. Bon voyage.

TOP RIGHT: Originally called Salle des Capucines because of its location on the Boulevard des Capucines, it became known as the Palais Garnier after its architect, Charles Garnier.

RIGHT: The Louvre pyramid entrance was designed by I. M. Pei to handle the huge number of tourists visiting France's most popular museum.

The Passage du Gois

France

Length: 4.3 km, 2.7 miles
Start: Beauvoir-sur-Mer
Finish: Isle de Noirmoutier
Highlights: The thrill of leaving your journey till the water is lapping…

Located to the south-west of the French town of Nantes, in the department of Vendée, is what may be the most impassable road in the world.

The causeway known as the Passage du Gois (or Gôa) is a 4.3-km-long road that joins the small coastal town of Beauvoir-sur-Mer to the low-lying island of Noirmoutier. The road is under water for 18 hours a day. At low tide, the stone paved surface of the causeway can be slippery, but this is not the main hazard that drivers must face. What makes this road so dangerous is that there are only two 3-hour windows each day in which the road lies above the surface of the water. For an hour and a half before and after each low tide, the causeway is passable. Outside that time period, the Atlantic tide rushes in and floods the road, covering it in seawater to depths of up to 4 metres (13 ft) at high tide.

People traversed the sandbanks between the island and the coast at Beauvoir on foot for many centuries, but it was not until the 18th century that the paved causeway was first built. A plaque at the Beauvoir end of the causeway celebrates a man called Gauvrit, who was the first to cross the causeway on horseback.

To help drivers stay safe, information panels are placed at each end of the causeway, giving the time of low tide each day as well as information about weather conditions. A number of rescue towers have been built along the causeway so that any drivers who are trapped by the tide can climb up above the height of the water and be rescued. Of course, the same cannot be said of their cars.

Parking on the causeway is forbidden, and drivers should be cautious about stray clumps of seaweed on the road surface, which make it slippery. Using the causeway in fog is strongly discouraged.

Nowadays, traffic is allowed to travel in only one direction across the causeway – from the mainland to the island. The French authorities have spoiled the fun by building a bridge to the island, and so the hazards of meeting French drivers coming the other way and indulging in stereotypical handwaving are gone. But even though it's one direction please remember – time and tide wait for no man.

OPPOSITE: Too late to start now, the route to the island is swallowed up by the incoming tide.

LEFT: For those unfortunate to be stranded, there is a refuge en route.

Portuguese Surfin' Safari

Portugal

Length: 825 km, 513 miles
Start: Porto
Finish: Faro
Highlights: Porto, Ribeira Square, Ericeira Beach, Lisbon, Sintra, Lagos, Sagres, Faro

This is one for the surfers; load up your campervan, grab the boards and start hunting for some of the best waves Europe has to offer. If you are not a surfer, Portugal is a country of great food and drink, spectacular ocean scenery, a rich history and welcoming and passionate people.

Start in the ancient city of Porto, a UNESCO World Heritage Site since 1996 and famous for its major export, port wine. It would be well worth spending a couple of nights in this gorgeous city. The train station alone is worth visiting, with over 20,000 tiles telling the history of Portugal. If you have a good head for heights take a trip across the Dom Luís I Bridge (pictured right) on foot or by tram. Take a tour around a port warehouse, stroll around the city market in Ribeira Square or just enjoy watching the evening sunset across the river with a glass of the city's namesake. This is a handsome, charismatic place.

When you feel ready to set off on your drive, head south towards Ericeira Beach. It's the venue for the Association of Surfing Professionals World Tour Championships and a mecca for anyone hunting consistent waves. Stop off at Figueira da Foz for some great bars and surf culture. But if you just can't wait that long for your surf fix, turn off down any dirt track towards the ocean from the N109 and you're bound to find your own private break.

After the town of Cascais, head for Lisbon, Portugal's beautiful capital city, with its distinctively relaxed atmosphere. For a true experience of local culture head for the Time Out Market, full of small shops and stalls offering a huge selection of the country's finest foods, including traditional custard tarts. There's something to suit all tastes. And you must take a ride on one of the city's famous yellow trams.

ABOVE RIGHT: There are three heritage tram lines in Porto running classic rolling stock.

RIGHT: The Dom Luís I Bridge over the Douro River in Porto.

OPPOSITE: A typical view on the drive south; deserted beaches and beckoning surf.

Take a drive out to Sintra to visit a former royal retreat in the Sintra Mountains. The Palace of Sintra, another UNESCO World Heritage Site, is the best-preserved medieval palace in Portugal. In Lisbon itself, visit one of Lisbon's most recognizable monuments, the Elevador de Santa Justa. This 19th-century elevator transports passengers from the Baixa district to the Largo do Carmo and the ruins of the Carmo church; but the real attraction is the panoramic views across the rooftops of Lisbon. If you are in need of more surf whilst in Lisbon try Carcavelos beach or Costa da Caparica just over the river.

When you've had your fill of Lisbon, head south on the A2 towards Sagres, driving through the Atlantic coastal countryside. For geological spectacles galore stop off at Ponta da Piedade, a stunning landscape of cliffs, sea caves, arches and grottos carved in golden-coloured rock. Dine on locally caught fish in Lagos, or the local speciality, conquilhas à Algarvia, clams cooked with onions, garlic and Portuguese sausage. Lagos has a beautiful walled Old Town and is renowned for its lively nightlife.

The coast west of Lagos towards Sagres is quiet and attractive, lined with fantastic beaches, and it shouldn't be too difficult to find a small bay all to yourself. For surf try Arrifana and Carrapateira. Sagres itself, at the end of both the west and south coasts of Portugal, has a pleasingly remote, laid-back atmosphere. Don't forget to take a trip out to Cabo Sao Vicente, the most southwesterly extremity of mainland Europe and, until the 14th century, considered the end

ABOVE LEFT: The Ribeira de ilhas beach, part of the Ericeira World Surfing Reserve. The *brahs* and *bettys* get *amped* and *frothing* over those *cranking* sets of waves.

TOP: A product of 19th-century romanticism, the Pena National Palace in Sintra.

ABOVE: Mercado da Ribeira, or Time Out Market in Lisbon.

of the known world! The views are spectacular and the history abounds: Henry the Navigator founded a nautical school here in around 1443, and in 1587 Sir Francis Drake successfully attacked Sagres fort.

For the final leg of your journey travel east along the coast to Faro. This stretch of coastline is an increasingly popular surfing destination. Praia da Rocha in the tourist resort of Portimão is one of the best beaches. The sands and villages along this stretch of coastline are magnificent and there is plenty of nightlife to be found. Faro is rich in history, abundant in Renaissance architecture and famous for its skeletons – in the medieval quarter you'll find the macabre Capela dos Ossos (Chapel of the Bones) in the 18th-century church of Nossa Senhora do Carmo.

Don't forget to fit in a last surf before heading home. At Praia de Faro there's a gentle break, perfect for beginners or those wanting a light cruise on a long board. Spend your last evening in the old town with a glass of local wine, watching the inhabitants go about their lives in one of the many cobbled plazas. Most visitors don't hang around this city, heading instead straight for the coastal resorts. They are missing out but it does mean the city has retained its authentic Portuguese feel. Now's the time to soak it up.

ABOVE: Ponta da Piedade rocks near Lagos.

Ring Road

Iceland

Length: 1,300 km, 800 miles
Start/Finish: Reykjavik
Highlights: Geysir, Gullfoss, Skogafoss, Svinafellsjökull, Jökulsarlon, Myvatn, Goðafoss, Akureyri

Iceland has a landscape like no other place in the world. Lying over an active fault in the earth's crust, it is still being formed by volcanic movement – a true land of ice and fire.

Iceland's geography has not had time to mellow like more ancient lands. Its ragged hills and mountains have not yet been rounded off by exposure to the elements. Its colourful soil is rich in minerals but not in organic matter. Its rivers are unpredictable and prone to sudden changes brought on by the interaction of glacial ice and volcanic fire. It is, once seen, unforgettable.

The Icelandic Ring Road is not a dangerous route, but it is important to be prepared for it. Outside the main towns of Reykjavik and Akureyri the country is sparsely populated. There can be long gaps between petrol stations, food stores and toilets. Know the distances you intend to cover, and carry water and other essentials with you.

Fuel, accommodation and refreshments are expensive in Iceland, so budget accordingly and plan ahead. At 2018 prices you can expect to spend $400 on petrol alone. Above all, choose the right vehicle for the job. Camper vans are available for hire in Reykavik and there is a good network of campsites along the Ring Road. If you are sticking to the Ring Road, any conventional urban car will make it. But if you venture off-piste, particularly inland, you'll find that many roads are little more than tracks bulldozed through the crumbling lava flows, and river crossings are fords, not bridges. Here, and everywhere in winter, four-wheel drive is essential.

This description takes the Ring Road anticlockwise, although either way is good; and it sticks to sites relatively close to the car. The road is easy to follow, Route 1 in the Icelandic road network and on signposts; and without detours and stops you could probably drive right round it in a couple of days. But what's a road trip without detours and stops?

An essential first detour is to leave Reykjavik not anticlockwise but heading northeast on Route 1 before turning right onto Route 36. This leads to the Þingvellir (pronounced Thing-vettleer) National Park, not only the site of the world's oldest parliament but a wonderful vantage point from which to observe the forces which continue to form this island. Rows of parallel fissures show

how Iceland is continually being widened by pressure from below, pushing the land outwards east and west.

Continue on Route 36 and turn left onto the 365, to arrive at Geysir, the place which gave its name to a natural phenomenon. Amidst a mosaic of pools coloured by the different minerals through which they spring, the geysers of Geysir and Strokkur are still very active. Further along the 365 this detour reaches its climax with the

magnificent waterfall of Gullfoss, the largest in Europe. As you will find, Foss is a common placename element, meaning Waterfall. If you've done the Golden Circle day trip from Reykjavik, you will already have seen these wonders. But if not, they are unmissable.

Turning back from Gullfoss, take Route 30 on your left and eventually turn left onto Route 1 in the direction of Hella. Look out for a small exhibition about one of Iceland's more recent

ABOVE: The 1,069-metre (3,507-ft) Búlandstindur mountain in Eastern Iceland.

OPPOSITE TOP: Strokkur is Iceland's most visited active geyser in the Geysir Geothermal Area. It blasts out every five-to-ten minutes. The term geyser is derived from Iceland's Geysir geyser which is currently inactive.

OPPOSITE BOTTOM: The Goðafoss waterfalls in North Central Iceland.

eruptions, Eyjafjallajökull (pronounced Eye-ah-fyattla-yerkool, it's the eruption that stopped worldwide flights in 2010) in a farmhouse on the left. A little further on, Skogafoss is a towering waterfall worth the short walk from the main road and familiar from several TV commercials.

Eventually the road curls down to the sea at the village of Vik (Vik, as in Reykjavik, means Township – Wick is the English equivalent). Vik is an important refuelling site, and on a walk around the headland to the west you will find a range of volcanic features including massive lava pillars and caves and Vik's celebrated black beach.

About an hour and a half beyond Vik, a short detour on Route 998 takes you to high, elegant Svartifoss; and back on Route 1 just beyond that, a turning to Svinafellsjökull. Jökull means glacier and here you can come face to face with one. In this volcanic landscape you may be disappointed to find that the white ice of glaciers is often blackened by the lava through which they carve. But it is nevertheless an awesome sight. This one is a tongue of the mighty Vatnajökull, around which the Ring Road now loops southwards.

Another tongue of Vatnajökull, Breiðarmerkurjökull, feeds the beautiful Jökulsarlon, right by the roadside. It's a lagoon filled with meltwater contained by the terminal moraine of the glacier, into which fragments of the glacier fall and float, like small icebergs.

Beyond the village of Hornafjörður the landscape changes. Iceland has spread out from its centre, and the east and west coasts exhibit the oldest geology in the country. The eastern region of Iceland is remote and sparsely populated. You will meet more sheep on the roads than cars. The Ring Road winds around several beautiful fjords before striking inland to the regional capital, Egilsstaðir. With a population of under 3,000 it grew up around a single farm of that name

and achieved town status only in 1947. From there Route 1 turns westwards, and northwards towards the Arctic Circle.

As the geology gets younger again, you enter the Hverir Geothermal Area, a region of high volcanic activity. At its centre is Myvatn ('Mee-vatten'), a lake which fills the fissures of an eruption which took place only 2,300 years ago – in geological terms that's barely yesterday. As you approach Myvatn, it's worth leaving the Ring Road to see Krafla, a spectacular volcano to the north; or, to the south, to swim in the Myvatn thermal pool.

The lake itself, a paradise for birdwatchers, is surrounded by the remains of volcanic vents – false craters where an erupting fissure has let off a little steam or lava. But a linguistic word of warning – Vatn means lake, and My means midge. The Lake of Midges lives up to its name in the summer months.

As you move on from Myvatn to the large northern town of Akureyri, watch out for a sign to Goðafoss, the Waterfall of the Gods, on the left. It's a short drive and short walk to this horseshoe-shaped wonder. Goðafoss gets its name from the legend that, following Iceland's conversion to Christianity, statues of the old Norse gods were thrown into the falls.

Akureyri is the second largest settlement in Iceland after Reykjavik. It has a relatively mild climate and owes its economic success to its icefree harbour, from which you can take whale-watching trips. It's a centre for Icelandic folk culture, and the Arctic Open Golf Tournament is played here every year on the Summer Solstice – which means golfers have the novelty of teeing off at 2am in the morning.

From Akureyri the road turns reluctantly towards Reykjavik. You pass through Varmahilð, whose name means 'warm hillside' – it's one of several

areas which take advantage of natural thermal energy to grow exotic fruit and vegetables unimaginable in a cold climate. Varmahilð is also a centre for breeding Icelandic ponies and for pony trekking. Further on, Blonduos has a striking modern church built in the shape of a volcano.

If you have time – a lot of time – it's worth exploring the grandeur of the Western Fjords via Routes 68, 61 and 60. And before you get back to Reykjavik, there's one last detour, into the Snaefellsnes peninsula. Turn right onto Route 54 at Borgames and you enter a landscape known as Iceland in Miniature. Snaefellsnes is the setting for one of the classic Icelandic sagas, and for Jules Verne's Voyage to the Centre of the Earth. It contains many classic Icelandic features – the Snaefellsnes glacier and volcano at its western end, several small fishing villages along its northern shore, and at Kirkjufell a striking conical mountain and a charming two-step waterfall.

Reykjavik, a modern, international capital, may come as a shock of bright lights and bustle after the otherworldliness of the Icelandic landscape. If you set off again immediately to repeat the Ring Road trip, you could do it without repeating any of the experiences you had already gathered. Painted hillsides; craters black, red and yellow with minerals; hot springs emerging from beneath ice-cold glaciers; barren wilderness and fertile plains. Iceland is a country so small that you can see the history of its creation from its Ring Road.

LEFT: Weather can change quickly in Iceland so real-time updates can be obtained from www.vegagerdin.is

TOP RIGHT: A Ring Road bridge over the river Jökulsá á Fjöllum.

RIGHT: The Aurora Borealis, or Northern Lights, seen over Akureyri in North Iceland.

The Road of Death

Bolivia

Length: 93 km, 58 miles
Start: La Paz
Finish: Coroico
Highlights: La Cumbre Pass, Rio Elena, Mono Zip-line, Coroico

When the Inter-American Development Bank declared the North Yungas Road in Bolivia to be the most dangerous road in the world in 1995, it became a magnet for thrill-seekers. Some 25,000 people now travel its precipitous route every year – just for fun.

Despite some of the stretches of this perilous road getting upgraded in 2006, it still claims the lives of up to 300 travellers a year, earning it the nickname Road of Death. Yungas is a band of rainforest on the north-eastern slopes of the Andes. It's an impenetrable area where the easiest way to get about is by zip wires strung above the valleys rather than paths down into and out of them. The regional centre, Coroico, was for a long time inaccessible from the Bolivian capital La Paz, only 56 km to the southwest as the condor flies.

In the 1930s Bolivia was fighting a territorial war with neighbouring Paraguay to the southeast and facing significant difficulties in supplying troops at the front. It used Paraguayan prisoners to improve its transport infrastructure by building a new road across the mountains to Coroico – the North Yungas Road.

'Build' is perhaps too strong a word. In many places it was simply hacked, barely wide enough for a single car, out of almost vertical cliffs, from which tall seasonal waterfalls fall directly onto the unpaved muddy surface, washing it away. In wet weather, rain and mist reduce visibility to dangerous levels; in dry weather the dust has the same effect. It is a hellish road, not one for the squeamish, anyone with a fear of heights, or confined spaces, the risk-averse, the novice driver, the impatient … for any of the above, just watching online videos of the road will be enough of a deterrent.

For the rest, the road leaves La Paz in relatively reassuring condition on Route 3 – surfaced, wide enough for several vehicles to pass each other unhindered, rising steadily through the suburbs and industrial zones of the city. La Paz, at 3,640 metres (11,942 ft), is the highest capital in the world. But over the next 23 km the road climbs another thousand metres to La Cumbre Pass, 4,650 metres (15,256 ft) above sea level. There's a lake here, Laguna Estrellani, and a tourist information centre; and it's here that bicycle tour groups from La Paz are delivered by minibus.

What follows may account for the popularity of this road trip among the cycling fraternity. The next 64 km are all downhill (apart from one tiny uphill stretch). From beyond the Pass the road follows the narrow valley of the Rio Pongo east for 20 km. The Pongo joins the Undavi and

TOP: Roadside memorials to those who have plunged over the edge are an all-too-familiar sight on the road.

ABOVE AND RIGHT: There is little or no room for error on the unbordered loose gravel surface.

where that river turns south an innocuous yellow sign announces in Spanish and English: 'DEATH ROAD – KEEP YOUR LEFT'. This is where the tarmac ends and the adventure begins.

As a nation, Bolivia drives on the right. The reason for making the Road of Death the exception is that it places the driver as near to the edge of the road as possible. Passing an oncoming vehicle on the narrow North Yungas Road is sometimes a matter of very fine judgement, and you want the driver most at risk of plummeting to his death to be as acutely aware of the margin for error as possible. The drop is not always as much as 600 metres (1,969 ft), but often it is. Sadly the next 40 km or so are punctuated with crosses and other memorials to those who miscalculated.

If you dare take your eyes off the road, the views are amazing, even in rainforest mist. Exotic foliage looms out of the clouds at you and even glimpses of the mountains around you and the densely forested valley of the Rio Elena below are exhilarating. Driving on the left as you descend you are clinging to the righthand side of the valley, hairpin bends twisting around its tributaries and out around their flanks. At one point the road actually runs behind a high waterfall spouting from the cliff above. And

further down at the Mono Zip-line and Café you can try travelling as the locals do, by high wire.

At a tourist control barrier the road eventually swings away from the Elena around a spur, reaching its lowest point as it crosses the Rio Yolosa, a mere 990 metres (3,248 ft) in altitude. From here it's a gentle 7-km climb to Coroico. It's a pretty town with a handsome square, jutting out on a spur of the mountains behind it, with plenty of history and hostels.

The modernization of the Road of Death between 1986 and 2006 included widening and the erection of safety barriers, and the most dangerous parts of the original road were bypassed by a new route to the north. For the first time trucks and buses had a road surface wider than their wheelbase on which to carry their trade between Coroico and La Paz. This new Yungas Road is 11 km longer than the old and as much as an hour faster to drive, but for a certain type of traveller, not nearly as much fun.

ABOVE: Drivers have to avoid trucks, buses and mobs of mountain bikers making the descent.

RIGHT: A panoramic view of the Camino de la Muerte leading down to Yungas, Coroico, Bolivia.

The Road to Tizi N'Test

Morocco

Length: 250 km, 155 miles
Start: Marrakech
Finish: Taroudant
Highlights: Imlil, Tinmel, Tizi N'Test, Taroudant

There are few better ways to get under the skin of this beguiling country than a trip exploring the Tizi N'Test pass – a road less travelled.

There's a new motorway heading south from Marrakech to Agadir and Taroudant. It makes the hot journey across the western flanks of the Atlas Mountains possible in around three hours. It also makes it straight and dull. The old route, with the perilous ascent and descent of the Tizi N'Test Pass, winds its way up and down the mountains through pretty villages, fertile valleys and age-old history.

Morocco is known for its ancient cities, colourful markets, stunning silver craftsmanship, Berber carpets, and the smell of jasmine wafting through the air on a warm evening. You will undoubtedly start and end your journey in Marrakech and staying a night or two here is certainly worth considering. This frenetic city, sitting on the edge of the Sahara desert, has a millennium of history to be enjoyed. The UNESCO heritage status gives some indication of the beauty to be found within this bustling city, but it is no museum and its modern entrepreneurism is clear.

Once you have had your senses well and truly bombarded by Marrakech, it is time to hit the road and head for the mountains on the R203. It is perhaps worth hiring a driver so you can enjoy

ABOVE: A distance marker near the Tizi N'Test Pass.

OPPOSITE: Viewed at a distance the climb to Tizi N'Test looks straightforward. It's not. And it's particularly tricky when it rains.

the sights of the surrounding landscape and relax in the knowledge that they can handle a road fairly described on the map as 'dangerous and difficult'.

Your first stop high in the Atlas Mountains is Imlil, a short drive off the main road. The desert heat of Morocco is exchanged for the crisp cool of a mountain village and views of the snow-capped Atlas Mountains. There are two things to do in Imlil: hike, or sit and relax with a refreshing mint tea enjoying the gentle comings and goings of the local Berber people. For the former, walk into the mountains to visit the local waterfalls, wander down into the fertile valley, or gear up to make the ascent to the top of Mount

Toubkal, which at 4,167 metres (13,671 ft) is the highest peak in North Africa.

When you are ready to begin your exploration of the interior of the Atlas Mountains, return to the main road and head southwest. Neat clusters of houses and small villages dot the hillsides, their earthy hues, softened in the mountain light, contrasting with bright green terraced gardens and the delicate blossoms of cherry trees.

After the village of Ouirgane all evidence of tourism will fade into the distance as you head for Tinmel. This unremarkable little village, easily missed if you are not paying attention, was the capital of the Almohad Empire in the

12th century. Its 1156 mosque still stands today, the oldest in Morocco and one of only two which may be visited by non-Muslims. It's a mesmerizing place of precisely aligned Moorish arches and not to be missed. This little village is a wonderful place to break for lunch with a strong, hot coffee and immerse yourself in rural Moroccan life.

It's only after Tinmel that the engineering brilliance of the R203 becomes apparent. Now the vegetation thins out and the road climbs steadily but gently, clinging to ridges and valleys to maintain height on its way to Tizi N'Test. Round every bend another magnificent panorama opens up. These are views on a giant scale.

At the summit, 2,093 metres (6,867 ft) up, is the isolated Auberge Restaurant La Haute Vue, with a souvenir shop and campsite. A plaque commemorates the French roadbuilders who made your journey possible. The views here are good in all directions; but a little further on La Belle Vue Hotel and Restaurant, standing within a hairpin bend at the start of your descent, offers a breathtaking look at the road and the landscape ahead. Row upon row of mountains lie beneath you, and the R203 seems to snake round every one of them.

It is a phenomenal road, both exhilarating and beautiful. The views around each hairpin bend will take your breath away as you follow the contours of the mountain, through a landscape of pink granite and vast rock formations, and slowly wind your way to the plains of the Souss valley far below.

Driving past orange groves, argan trees and rooftops strewn with hibiscus and bougainvillea, you will be greeted by the 15th-century ochre-coloured, red-mud ramparts of the city of Taroudant. If you can time your drive to approach the city during the golden hour, just before sunset, you won't be disappointed. While in Taroudant, enjoy a ride in a horse-drawn calèche, barter for almonds, and watch the sunset from the city walls.

Taroudant owes its wealth to its position on the trade route over which you have driven; and today it still boasts both Berber and Arab markets. It is almost completely untouched, and unmoved, by tourism. Rest a while here soaking up the colour of this unspoilt city before you return to Marrakech. By motorway, if you prefer.

OPPOSITE TOP: At the top of Tizi N'Test you can buy a traditional Moroccan tagine.

OPPOSITE BOTTOM: A typical Berber village on the road to Taroudant.

RIGHT: This was the first road to link Marakech with the Souss plains. The road was blasted out of the rock by French engineers in 1929.

BELOW: The 6-kilometre-long walls of Taroudant, a city known as the 'Grandmother of Marakech'.

Romantic Road

Germany

Length: 400 km, 249 miles
Start: Würzburg
Finish: Füssen
Highlights: Würzburg, Rothenburg ob der Tauber, Dinkelsbühl, Nördlingen, Landsberg am Lech, Neuschwanstein

Germany's Romantic Road evokes an old image of the country – medieval villages with their market squares and churches, hills and lakes for healthy outdoor pursuits, forests and mountains to feed the wild, noble spirit.

The Romantic Road – die Romantische Strasse – was devised in the 1950s as a means of reviving tourism in Germany after World War Two. It explores the south-west of the country in the regions of Bavaria (Bayern) and Baden-Württemberg, avoiding major cities and concentrating on the spaces in between. Although most of the charming villages on the route have expanded in the past 60 years, the Romantic Road encouraged the idea that their beautiful old centres were worth preserving. Their medieval cores still survive therefore for the pleasure of future visitors.

The route begins in Würzburg, a lively university town dominated by the Marienberg fortress, mostly dating from the 17th century. Germany's approach to its architectural heritage has been to reconstruct buildings from their ruins. So in Würzburg, which was flattened by the RAF during World War Two, you can once again see baroque gems like the Falkenhaus and the old bridge over the River Main.

Try the local Franconian wine (Frankenwein). Bavaria is famous for its beer festivals, but Frankenwein is delicious and rarely found outside the region. It is traditionally sold in the distinctive Bocksbeutal, a flagon-like bottle with the profile of a large table-tennis bat.

Head west first, to Wertheim, at the confluence of the Main and the Tauber west of Würzburg. The Romantische Strasse was expanded in 2016 to include Wertheim, which earns its place with a dramatic red sandstone castle above a half-timbered medieval centre.

Following the Tauber upstream the Road arrives in Rothenburg ob der Tauber, considered the most complete medieval town in Germany. It retains its old town walls and nearby is an unusual bridge over the now-narrow river. Its double-decker rows of arches were originally built in 1330.

ABOVE RIGHT: Würzburg on the river Main in Bavaria.

RIGHT: Looking towards the Markus clock tower in Rothenburg ob der Tauber.

OPPOSITE: The narrow, timber-framed building in Rothenburg ob der Tauber is known as Das Plönlein. It is flanked by the Kobolzeller Tower and the higher Siebers Tower.

Crossing the Franconian Heights the road continues through Feuchtwangen, whose old marketplace is so grand and lively that it was described in the 19th century as Franconia's ballroom. Dinkelsbühl on the southern edge of the Heights has well-preserved town walls built in 1305. Its surrender to the Swedish Army in 1632 during the Thirty Years War is celebrated every year with gifts of sweets to children, because a young Dinkelsbühl girl so reminded a Swedish officer of his own daughter that he spared the town.

Further south, Nördlingen is the third of only three German towns (with Rothenburg and Dinkelsbühl) to retain its complete defensive ring of walls. The circular plan of the original town, built within an ancient impact crater, is still evident. Spared intensive bombing during World War Two, much of Nördlingen's medieval centre is original, not reconstructed. Outside the walls the town also houses the Bavarian Railway Museum.

The Romantische Strasse now follows the Wörnitz river south to Harburg. This little village has a big castle, Burg Harburg, on which construction began before 1150. Never damaged by wars, it remains a model of medieval defensive

architecture with its many towers, so perfect that Michael Jackson is said to have tried, unsuccessfully, to buy it. It is still the property of the princely House of Öttingen-Wallerstein.

The Wörnitz joins the Danube at Donauwörth. The route crosses the Danube here and travels on to the city of Augsburg. Founded in 15 BC by the Romans, Augsburg is the third oldest town in Germany. It has architectural relics of every era since then, and a scale, maturity and grandeur in marked contrast to the rural centres through which the Romantische Strasse has passed so far. Don't miss the Perlachturm, a belltower from 989 AD, and the Fuggerei, a walled town-within-a-town built in 1516 for the needy and vulnerable of Augsburg.

Augsburg sits on the River Lech, another tributary of the Danube; and the Romantic Road follows the Lech upstream for the rest of the journey. Landsberg am Lech was an important crossing of the river on an ancient salt-trading route. It has several impressive town gates,

ABOVE: An ancient bridge over the River Wörnitz in Harburg.

RIGHT: The village centre in Bad Mergentheim. Beethoven played viola in the court orchestra here in 1791.

especially the one through which travellers from Munich arrived. The town was briefly notorious as the place where Adolf Hitler wrote *Mein Kampf* while in prison for treason.

At Steingaden, 20 km north of Füssen, there's a magnificent rococo church with an oval ground plan. It was built for pilgrims to the town after tears were said to have appeared on a wooden sculpture of Christ in 1732. Füssen itself marks the southern end of the Romantische Strasse, close to the borders with Switzerland and Austria, and the principality of Liechtenstein. It sits at the head of the Forggensee lake through which the Lech flows, and is ringed by four other lakes. Its town centre is dominated by the Hohes Schloss, a summer palace of the Bishops of Augsburg.

The composer Richard Wagner used to stay here when he visited mad King Ludwig II at the king's summer residence nearby, the wonderful fairytale castle of Neuschwanstein. This epitome of the romantic ideal of a castle, on a mountaintop surrounded by forest, was built on the site of two real medieval castles which were demolished to make way for it. It was the inspiration for Disney's Sleeping Beauty Castle and the location for the filming of *Chitty Chitty Bang Bang*. It is astonishingly beautiful, and a fitting finale to the Romantische Strasse.

ABOVE LEFT: Half-timbered houses lining the streets of Dinkelsbühl. Dinkelsbühl, along with Rothenburg ob der Tauber and Nördlingen are three German towns on the route that still retain their complete city walls.

ABOVE: Mad King Ludwig's fairytale castle Neuschwanstein was completed in 1886. It was built over the ruins of two medieval castles and was partly a retreat for Ludwig II and partly a tribute to composer Richard Wagner.

Route des Grandes Alpes

France

Length: 688 km, 427 miles
Start: Thonon-les-Bains
Finish: Menton
Highlights: Cascade de Dard, Col de l'Iseran, Bonneval-sur-Arc, Esseillon forts, Forte du Télégraphe, Col du Galibier, Briançon, Forte de Tournoux, Saint-Martin-Vésubie, Col de Turini, Sospel

Popular with cyclists due to its associations with the Tour de France, the Route des Grandes Alpes is a gruelling test for any machine, and the person steering it. Even if you don't have to pedal.

From the shore of Lake Geneva to the coast of the French Riviera, this signposted route crosses every single high mountain pass in the French Alps. This is a trip to delight lovers of hairpin bends, crumbling fortresses, remote villages and mountains, but can only be attempted once the snows of winter have passed.

Over a dozen alpine passes are connected by a route originally devised in 1909 to improve access to the isolated communities of this eastern region of France. It became a vital lifeline for them and for France's defence of her

borders in World War One. The expansion of the French motorway network has reduced the flow of traffic on the Route des Grandes Alpes. Its attraction for drivers who like a challenge remains undiminished. It will take you and your car several days to complete the whole route, and even experienced alpine cyclists will need more than a week.

Self-evidently this is a landscape shaped by ice and snow. The meltwater torrent of the the Dranse River for example has scoured out the extraordinary rock forms of the Gorge

du Pont-du-Diable, just 15 km from the starting point Thonon-les-Bains.

Further upriver you'll pass the ruins of Aulps Abbey before arriving at the village of Morzine. This, France's most northerly alpine resort, is divided by another gorge on the same river. From here the route takes on its first serious challenge, the Col de la Colombière. Over 16 km the road climbs 1,108 metres (3,635 ft) to the summit at 1,613 metres (5,292 ft).

On the next, Col des Aravis, sits the pretty Chapel of St Anne, a saint who protects travellers beneath the cliffs of the Aravis mountain range. On your descent from here, don't miss the Cascade de Dard, a high waterfall above a deep gorge into which you can walk down a wooden staircase.

Where there are mountains there are often lakes. On your zig-zag way up to the Cormet de Roselend pass you'll pass Roselend Reservoir, and later on the route Lac de Chevril. It conceals the old village of Tignes which was submerged to create it. Although you can't plan your trip around it, you may be lucky enough to see Tignes, which is revealed once every ten years when they drain the water for routine maintenance.

Above Chevril is the skiing resort of Val d'Isère and above that the Col de l'Iseran, at 2,770 metres (9,088 ft) the highest paved pass in the Alps. Even with gradients of up to 12 per cent the road makes use of tunnels and galleries to snake its way over and down again. During your descent alongside the Arc River you'll pass through the beautiful alpine village of

TOP: The route takes in many of the high passes or *cols* of the Alps and so fans of the Tour de France will find some very familiar names, along with sweaty, lycra-clad *grimpeurs* (climbers) on bikes.

ABOVE: Like the majority of roads in France, the route is very well signposted.

Bonneval-sur-Arc, an unspoilt gem of traditional alpine architecture.

Soon the route climbs again, to cross the Esseillon Barrier via the Col du Mont Cenis. This rocky ridge is defended by a line of five French forts built in the mid-19th century for a coming war with the neighbouring Kingdom of Sardinia. The war never materialized and the only action the forts ever saw was as prisons during World War Two. At the next pass, Col du Télégraphe, another dramatic fortress with two drawbridges did fire its guns in anger, at the invading Italian army in 1940.

The Col du Télégraphe, and the Col du Galibier to its south, are two of the most familiar mountain stages in the Tour de France. The latter is marked by a memorial to the race's first director, Henri Desgranges. Until 1976 the terrain at Galibier was considered so bad that no road could go over the top of it. Instead a tunnel ran through the rock.

Pass follows pass. The Col de Montgenèvre was a key link between France and Turin. The town of Briançon which guards it is now a UNESCO World Heritage Site for its fortifications. Beyond the steep Col d'Izoard the road is cut into the rock as it follows the canyons of the Guil River.

Above the Col de Vars, the Forte de Tournoux is built into the steep hillside like a Himalayan monastery. The hairpin bends required to reach it were so sharp that carts would topple as they turned them. To avoid this, they simply didn't turn: instead, they stopped, unhitched the mules and rehitched them at the rear of the cart on duplicate shafts. Further south again, beyond the Col de la Couillole, you can see remnants of the Maginot Line, built between world wars to defend France's eastern borders.

As the route passes from the Alps to the Mediterranean it goes through charming, cobbled, narrow-streeted villages like Saint-Sauveur-sur-Tinée and Saint-Martin-Vésubie before climbing one last pass, the Col de Turini, whose hairpin bends are famous as a stage of the Monte Carlo Rally. From here the Route des Grandes Alpes descends slowly, through historic Sospel with its 13th-century toll bridge,

to coastal Menton, the last town on the French Riviera before Italy. From 2,770 metres (9,088 ft) above sea level, to sea level – this is a trip of no lows and many highs.

OPPOSITE: The route is only possible/passable in the summer months. Many of the high cols are snowbound and the road to one, Col de la Madeleine (though not on the route) is a numbered and pisted ski slope.

ABOVE: La Chapelle des Aravis en route to the Col des Aravis in the Haute-Savoie, near La Clusaz.

TOP RIGHT: Col du Galibier, near Valloire, is often the highest pass of the Tour de France.

RIGHT: Col de L'Iseran, near Tignes, is the highest pass on a metalled road in France.

Route 66: Ash Fork to Topock

Arizona, USA

Length: 162 miles, 260 km
Start: Ash Fork
Finish: Topock
Highlights: Seligman, Hackberry, Kingman, Sitgreaves Pass, Oatman

This would have been a remarkable road trip for thousands of families heading for California to escape the dustbowls of the Midwest. Today it is hard to imagine how they made it in 1930s boneshakers…

Ask anyone to name a classic road trip and chances are they will come up with Route 66, the 2,450-mile highway traversing eight states from Chicago in Illinois to Santa Monica, in California. Bobby Troup made it famous in his song, getting his kicks on Route 66 and naming some of the places along the way.

It passes through Illinois, Missouri, Kansas, Oklahoma, Texas, New Mexico, Arizona and California before it reaches journey's end; however, there are only 22 miles of Route 66 in Kansas, which is left out of the song. The highway was first designated in 1926 and hooked up a number of local roads and pre-existing trails, to give a route for many families heading west to the land of opportunity, California. Even today, most tourists travel from east to west, but the road has long been superseded by the I-44 and

I-40 which track what is now termed Historic Route 66 for much of the journey.

But whereas the 'Mother Road' goes right through towns and cities, the Interstate dodges round, and in some parts of the country takes a widely diverging route. Because Route 66 was never expected to survive much beyond the 1970s, it has gradually been dismantled after the Interstate took over. In the case of Glenrio, Texas, the wide carriageway of four lanes has been left

RIGHT: Vintage Route 66 exiting Kingman and heading off, through many river washes to the Sitgreaves Pass.

BELOW: The resurrection of Historic Route 66 owes a debt to the Delgadillo Brothers of Seligman.

to service local houses, but beyond the ghost town of derelict motels and garages, it peters out into a single gravel road and then disappears into desert.

The last section to exist, around Flagstaff, Arizona, was officially delisted in 1984 and singer Bobby Troup was there to witness the signs coming down. However the state Historic Route 66 associations have pieced together a route from Chicago to Santa Monica using various different alignments of the route through its history.

The longest stretch of original, unblemished Route 66 runs through Arizona to the California border, and includes some of the most spectacular scenery it has to offer. Branching off the I-40 a few miles east of Ash Fork, the road heads for Seligman, home of the Delgadillo Brothers who were instrumental in the renaissance of Route 66. When the Interstate

bypassed their town, they weren't prepared to see it die and helped start up the first state association to resurrect the route.

Juan Delgadillo's Snow Cap café is on the left as you drive into town, with Angel Delgadillo's gift shop and information centre fifty yards further on. Beyond the many 'roadside attractions' of Seligman, including the Roadkill Café, the road passes along the valley through Peach Springs and Truxton to Hackberry and its general store. The ramshackle collection of old cars, gas pumps, metal signs and artefacts make it look like an autojumble with a gift shop attached, and it is a compulsory stop for all Route 66ers. It was set up by hippie artist Bob Waldmire in the 1990s, who became the inspiration for the character 'Filmore' in the Disney movie *Cars*.

The road continues to Kingman, passes by the railroad depot and the old Hotel Beale, briefly paralleling the I-40 for a few miles south of

BELOW LEFT: Outside, the Hackberry General Store resembles an autojumble where nothing is for sale. Inside, everything is for sale.

BELOW: Hackberry was revamped by celebrated Route 66 hippy artist Bob Waldmire.

BOTTOM: In the 1930s, motorists would pay locals to drive their cars up this hill.

BELOW RIGHT: The Cool Springs gas station was destroyed by fire in 1966, rebuilt for the film *Universal Soldier* in 1991 and then blown up by the film crew. It was reconstucted in its original form in 2002.

the town, before cutting west. The Oatman Road is long and straight and the perfect place to take classic Route 66 photos, as the old road heads through an arid landscape towards infinity, with the distant imposing backdrop of the Black Mountains.

The road passes through many dried-up river beds or 'washes' before it begins to climb towards Cool Springs, the site of a classic,

restored gas station with the striking 'Squaw's Teat' mountain beyond. Further up the slope is one of the unrestored relics of the old road; Ed's Camp was a place to park up, camp and buy water, or sleep in a screened bed for a dollar a night, before attempting the big climb to Sitgreaves Pass. Today it is protected from souvenir hunters by barbed wire, but the business closed in 1978 and has been left very much as it was abandoned.

Up until 1952, when the road was bypassed, cars struggled up the narrow, twisting track to the highest point of the route in Mohave County. Driving the perfectly metalled road today with all the convenience of power steering, sophisticated suspension and automatic transmission it is difficult to imagine boneshaker vehicles of only a few horsepower, and gearboxes that needed double de-clutching making it up a rutted gravel route, but there was no other way. In fact the

drive was so difficult that a business was set up to tow cars over the pass, or locals could be hired to drive strangers' cars for them.

Reaching the top at Sitgreaves Pass, there are places to park up and gaze down towards the old workings of the Goldroad Mine, including a place for impromptu 'murals and memorials'. From here it is downhill into Oatman, the most extraordinary town on the entire length of 66. The fortunes of Oatman have fluctuated with the discovery of gold nearby in 1908, and another vein in 1915. After the gold ran out, Route 66 brought a steady stream of traffic through until 1952, when six of the seven gas stations closed down overnight. It was then used and adapted for the movie set of *How The West Was Won* in 1961 and still retains some of the wooden boardwalks.

Today Oatman is a tourist destination with many visitors coming to see and feed the packs of wild burros roaming the streets. When the miners left town they abandoned their donkeys, which have survived and thrived and amble about the main street, mixing it with packs of German bikers on hired Harley Davidsons, making the classic American road trip.

FAR LEFT: Olive Oatman, the lady in the photo over the door, was captured by Native Americans in 1851 at the age of 14 and sold to the Mohave as a slave. She was released five years later. Oatman is named after this extraordinary woman.

LEFT: Burros roam the streets of Oatman and will try and eat most things, including Harley-Davidson aerials.

ABOVE: The Oatman Hotel, where Clark Gable and Carole Lombard supposedly spent their wedding night.

From Oatman it is almost all downhill to Topock on the Oatman-Topock Highway and beyond to the Colorado River bridge and California. A few miles south of Oatman, Historic 66 curves to the left following the mountains. Drivers can choose to go straight on to Mesquite and the Fort Mojave Reservation, or keep following the route that John Steinbeck vividly described for the Joad family in his classic book *The Grapes of Wrath*.

Route 66 has many more highlights in store before it reaches Santa Monica, but it is this section between Kingman and Oatman that leaves the most lasting impression of the 2,450 miles, a combination of wonderful scenery and the ghosts of epic journeys past.

Route des Vins d'Alsace

France

Length: 170 km, 106 miles
Start: Thann
Finish: Marlenheim
Highlights: Eguisheim, Colmar, Riquewihr, Ribeauvillé, Châtenois, Barr, Obernai

Established in 1953, and now the most famous wine route in France, the Alsace Wine Route passes through 70 wine-producing villages, skirting the foothills of the Vosges Mountains. It is, if you like, the road trip that drives you to drink.

The wine route began its life as a popular touring rally. It stretches for 170 km from the town of Thann in the south to Marlenheim in the north. Naturally, many people follow the route in order to sample wine and fine food at some of the villages on the way, or to attend wine festivals. However, the route is also remarkable for passing through stunning medieval villages and areas of great natural beauty. On many stretches of the route, the road runs directly through the vineyards from which the wine is produced, a rare experience on other wine trails.

The road is signposted with signs in white on brown which show a bunch of grapes and a wine glass and the words 'route des vins d'Alsace'. If there's any doubt about which way to go, just stay off main roads, keep the Vosges foothills on your left and the open Plein d'Alsace on your right, and you won't go far wrong. The driving is generally easy, following narrow D-roads through gently undulating countryside covered with a patchwork of vineyards and field of other crops.

The trip is not unduly busy in any season, but is at its most scenic from May to September, when the grapes and leaves are still on the vines. You will want to spend a few days driving, and a few evenings drinking, on the route. Harvest season is in October, and access to some vineyards may be prohibited during that time.

RIGHT: The Church of Sainte-Hune near the village of Hunawihr, voted one of the most beautiful villages in France.

The most dramatic scenery and the most beautiful historic villages are situated in the section between Thann and Obernai. Starting out from Thann, the route runs north for about 49 km to the town of Colmar, passing through two dozen wine-producing villages on the way. How to choose the prettiest of them? Eguisheim is representative of many. Like others along the route it takes the form of a circular walled village, having developed around a castle of the Duke of Alsace. Its narrow cobbled streets and central square are picture-postcard-perfect, and in 2013 it was voted France's Favourite Village.

Colmar was founded in the 9th century and, along with the rest of Alsace, has changed hands between France and Germany many times since then; a history which has resulted in some very un-French placenames, and a pleasing variety of architectural styles and cultural and culinary influences. The town boasts several interesting churches and museums and a beautiful area of half-timbered houses overlooking a canal. On summer evenings, the buildings are illuminated and the town certainly merits an overnight stay.

North of Colmar the road passes through the hilliest and most picturesque section of the route. The medieval walled village of Riquewihr, with its cobbled streets, half-timbered houses and open wine cellars, is another beautiful Alsatian enclave. Ribeauvillé is a medieval gem overlooked by not one but three ruined castles set among vineyards that climb the sides of the surrounding hills. This attractive town features colourful half-timbered houses and a Renaissance fountain in the main square. In a nearby forest stands the tallest sequoia outside the US, planted in 1856.

Châtenois has a different feel to other villages on the route. A disastrous fire in 1879 burnt down most of its timbered buildings, giving it the chance to rebuild in tune with the times. The Church of St George is particularly unusual for the region. One building which survived the

TOP: Looking down on the village of Riquewihr. The cobbled streets of the town are filled with wine cellars and tasting rooms.

LEFT: The Tour d'Eglise in Riquewihr. Elsewhere there is the Tour des Voleurs which has a collection of torture instruments.

ABOVE: Flowing through the centre of Vieux Colmar is La Lauch river.

OPPOSITE: The inner courtyard of Joseph Freudenreich et Fils winery in Eguisheim.

fire is the Witches' Tower built in 1432 and now crowned with a stork's nest. Many European folk traditions believe that a nesting stork confers good fortune on a village, and you will sometimes see artificial nests on poles, raised in the hope of attracting the birds.

North of Châtenois, you eventually reach Barr, the self-crowned wine capital of Alsace. It holds the oldest wine fair, and an exuberant harvest festival every October. Alsatian wine is considered alongside German wine, partly because both regions shared the transport facilities of the River Rhine. Alsace wine must be sold in bottles with tapering necks known as Rhine wine bottles. Best known for its aromatic Gewurztraminer and dry Riesling whites, about 10% of the region's production is in reds.

As you near the end of the Route you arrive in Obernai where – whisper it – they make beer as well as wine. Nevertheless the home of Kronenbourg lager is a beautiful town with some fine Renaissance architecture including an unusual six-bucket stone well. Marlenheim marks the northern end of the Route des Vins d'Alsace, nestled appropriately at the foot of the vine-covered eastern slopes of the Vosges.

This is a delightful road trip through a region much shaped by the shifting borders of Europe. Often the battleground for wider struggles like the Thirty Years War and World War Two, Alsace has almost miraculously retained a medieval charm. And that's worth raising a glass to.

La Ruta Panoramica

Puerto Rico

Length: 238 km, 148 miles
Start: Maunabo
Finish: Mayagüez
Highlights: Charco Azul, Cañon de San Cristobal, Toro Negro National Forest, Adjuntas, Maricao

La Ruta Panoramica splices together some of the secondary roads of Puerto Rico which weave along the mountain spine of the country, taking you far from the beaten track. You will encounter a traditional way of life in an enchanted but little known landscape.

Puerto Rico was ceded to the US from Spain in 1899 after the Spanish-American War. Columbus first gave the island the name of San Juan, with its capital named as Puerto Rico, 'the Rich Port'. Due to cartographic errors, this was reversed and so the island became 'Rich Port' and the capital San Juan. Informally, Spaniards came to call it the Island of Enchantment. This then is the island whose Panoramic Route will cast a spell over you.

You can drive it in either direction, but going from east to west you'll have the sun at your back and, as your surroundings become ever more rural, the sense of leaving the modern world behind. The route twists and turns its way through the mountains and can be slow and tiring to drive. You should aim to take two or three days over it, savouring the evenings spent out of your car as much as the hours spent in it.

The church of San Isidro Labrador in the south-eastern town of Maunabo marks the start of the route. Maunabo is separated from the rest of Puerto Rico by the chain of mountains to the north, and has preserved its own unique character as a result. A short climb, soon to be replaced by a tunnel, snakes up to the pass below Cerro La Pandura before the road descends to the farming town of Yabucoa, founded on land donated to the peasants in the 18th century by the ruling Spanish family.

After Yabucoa, follow the Rio Guayanés upstream through the scattered villages to its north. The Ruta turns north eventually to hop across hidden valleys towards the town of Espino, then heads westward again. It climbs up to Cerro de Nuestra Madre where you enter Bosque Estatal de Carite – the first of four national forest parks along the route. There are trails and campsites here, and the luminous blue of the waterfall-fed swimming hole at Charco Azul.

From here the Ruta Pamoramica rides along the Cordillera Central, the spine of Puerto Rico. It is certainly no straight line. This 240-km route is compressed into an island which at its longest is 180 km from end to end. It is, it must be said, intermittently sign-posted with distinctive brown 'RUTA' signs: take a map and a SatNav, but it will do you no harm to get lost occasionally. How far wrong can you go on an island only 65 km wide?

Although the route passes through few towns, most towns near it have gas stations.

The Ruta curls around the eastern slopes of Cerro Lucero and the southern edge of Lago Carite, one of 17 man-made lakes in Puerto Rico. Bypassing central Cayey it approaches Aibonito, the highest town in Puerto Rico where, in 1911,

ABOVE: Aibonito Cathedral.

OPPOSITE: View from the Ruta Panoramica deep in the Cordillera Central, the mountain range that runs along the centre of Puerto Rico.

the coldest temperature ever recorded in the country was experienced – 3 degrees above freezing. Between proud Aibonito and charming Barranquitas the road passes the western end of the Cañon de San Cristobal Nature Reserve, where a series of beautiful waterfalls and swimming holes leads to the deep blue canyon itself. Although it is not far, trails are unmarked and you are advised to use a local guide to find this natural highlight of the trip.

In the centre of the island the road passes through the Toro Negro National Forest, home to rare species including the Puerto Rican Broad-Winged Hawk. There are waterfalls and swimming holes with picnic areas here among the trees, and rising above the canopy is Cerro de Punta, Puerto Rico's tallest mountain at 1,338 metres (4,390 ft) high. You can drive most

TOP: Don't rely on finding signposts to guide you.

ABOVE LEFT: The entrance to the Dona Juana recreation area in the Toro Negro State Forest (Bosque Estatal).

LEFT: A view looking towards the Cordillera from the main square in Adjuntas.

of the way up and take a short walk to the summit for a panoramic overview of the entire island.

West of here, Adjuntas is an undiscovered little town with fine old haciendas in the surrounding hills. The discovery of gold and copper in the area has stirred strong local environmental concerns and Casa Pueblo in the town is a centre for ecological exhibitions and activism. Puerto Rico has become increasingly aware of the value of its natural assets since the 1970s, when the Ruta Panoramica was first defined.

At the western end of the Cordillera Central hangs the town of Maricao, built on the booming coffee trade of the 19th century. Although Puerto Rican beans now occupy only a small global niche, Maricao remains a centre for coffee growers in the region and the end of the harvest is celebrated in an annual festival. The small town gets its name from a local species of tree with yellow flowers, and has given its name to the nearby National Forest. From it the Ruta Panoramica drops gently down from the mountains to Plaza Colón in the coastal city of Mayagüez – not far from where Christopher Columbus landed on his second voyage to the Americas.

ABOVE: The town hall in Adjuntas.

RIGHT: A statue of Christopher Columbus, complete with fountains, commands the square in Mayagüez in front of Our Lady of Candelaria Cathedral.

Salar de Uyuni

Bolivia/Chile

Length: 500 km, 310 miles
Start: Uyuni, Bolivia
Finish: San Pedro de Atacama, Chile
Highlights: Train Cemetery, Cactus Island, Árbol de Piedra, Eduardo Avaroa Reserve, Sol de Mañana, Polques Hot Springs

Crossing the vast, wind-blasted plain of Bolivia's Salar de Uyuni is not for the faint-hearted. At 3,600 metres (11,811 ft) above sea level altitude sickness can be a problem, the UV is fierce and the sun's glare is reflected by the salt. By contrast, the night-time temperature can drop to 20°C below zero.

Need to get away from it all? At 12,000 square kilometres Salar de Uyuni is the world's largest salt plain and one of the planet's more remote locations. You are unlikely to bump into your neighbours. There are few roads in the area – none on the actual salar – so a well-maintained, four-wheel-drive vehicle is recommended. Carry plenty of fuel and water.

From December to April, rainfall sits on top of the salt and forms shallow lakes. These create a stunning mirror effect with the sky but can also render some areas swampy and impassable. The salt is not kind to cars and breakdowns are common so a little mechanical know-how is an advantage. Driving this region is an adventure but one which rewards the adventurous. Most visitors choose to explore it on an organized tour with 4x4 and a local driver. Visitors are advised to shop around to find a reliable operator.

A classic route starts from the town of Uyuni on the eastern edge of the salt plain. The drive heads west into the centre of the salar and then plunges south through high-altitude deserts to end at San Pedro de Atacama, a town on a plateau in the beautiful Andes mountains of north-eastern Chile. The distance between the two towns is 300 km as the condor flies, but most travellers rack up a figure closer to 500 km as they zigzag to take in the surrounding area's most interesting features.

RIGHT: The salt hotel, the Hotel de Sol Playa Blanca in Altiplano.

OPPOSITE: Heading into infinity on the world's largest salt flat, the Salar de Uyuni is what remains of a great prehistoric lake.

Intrepid visitors can look forward to smouldering vents, deserts, daunting mountains, geysers, hot springs and multicoloured lakes. It is a spectacular, volcanic landscape but also an unforgiving one. As a result, the flora and fauna are limited but what exists there is extraordinary. Giant cacti, meandering camelids and flocks of flamingo make for memorable photos. And while the lure of the salt plain is strong, the train cemetery at Uyuni is worth delaying your start for. It is included in the itinerary of most tours that run from Uyuni. Located 3 km out of town, it is a rusty graveyard for old locomotives that became obsolete when the nitrate mining industry collapsed in the 1940s.

The salt plain, or salar, is all that is left of the prehistoric lake Minchin. The salt is harvested and evidence of the industry is visible. Away from the works, the glowing, white, hexagonal salt tiles seem infinite. Mountains are visible in the far distance but they look unreal and appear to float above the endless, flat whiteness. The extreme flatness plays tricks with perspective. This lends itself to trompe l'oeil picture opportunities such as expedition vehicles being held in the palm of a hand. More usefully, the plain is so flat that it is used to calibrate the altimeters of satellites. Clear skies and a lack of light pollution mean that star-gazing visitors will feel as though they are in the heavens.

Breaking the horizon in the centre of the salar is Inca Huasi Island, also known as Cactus Island. A raised volcanic outcrop, it is covered in giant cacti and fossil coral formations which hark back to the area's watery past. Although rain sometimes makes it unreachable, it is a popular stop on the salar and has its own visitor centre.

From Inca Huasi, many head southwest to the desert regions of Chiguana and then Siloli. The Chilean border runs through this region. Glowering on the Chilean side, the fumaroles of the massive Ollagüe volcano constantly vent

sulphurous gases. Ollagüe is also responsible for the area's intriguingly shaped volcanic rocks. Curiously, the most famous rock formation in the area is el Árbol de Piedra which is made from sandstone rather than volcanic rock. Sculpted by the wind and sand, it is a precarious-looking, 7-metre-high, stone tree which rises from the sands of the southern edge of the Siloli desert.

Volcanic activity is very much evident in three of this region's lakes: Laguna Cañapa, Laguna Honda and Laguna Hedionda. Borax, sulphur and copper colour the land and water here as well as giving everything a distinct eggy odour. This does not stop three varieties of flamingo, including the rare James flamingo, from dropping by.

More flamingos can be seen at the Laguna Colorado in the Eduardo Avaroa Reserve.

The birds like the plankton which breed in the red water. Those who prefer their lakes green, should head to Laguna Verde, an emerald green body of water at the foot of the imposing but walkable Licancabur volcano. If your geological thirst has yet to be slaked then the geysers of Sol de Mañana or the thermal pools at Polques Hot Springs are worth exploring.

From the springs it is just under a 100-km drive across the border to San Pedro de Atacama. It is a small town which will seem like an oasis of comfort and sophistication after the adventure of the previous days.

OPPOSITE: The vast white expanse of the Salar de Uyuni viewed from Isla Incahuasi, the cactus field island in the middle of the salt flats.

ABOVE: It may not look promising for diversions, but there is an impressive cemetery of abandoned trains near Uyuni.

Southern Scenic Road

South Island, New Zealand

Length: 834 km, 518 miles
Start: Dunedin
Finish: Queenstown
Highlights: Nugget Point, Pūrākaunui Falls, Cathedral Caves, Te Hikoi Southern Journey, Lake Manapouri, Te Anau Caves, Milford Sound

The Southern Scenic Route was the first designated tourist drive in New Zealand, and its development over 25 years has produced an unforgettable trip through the southern end of South Island taking in lakes, mountains and of course the dramatic coastline.

The SSR encompasses diverse landscape, wildlife and the cultural heritage of New Zealand. Officially the route from Dunedin to Queenstown is 610 km in length. The drive can be undertaken at any time of the year, and makes a comfortable four-day break. Take a week over it and give yourself time to enjoy Queenstown and Dunedin too. Dunedin (the name is the Scottish Gaelic form of Edinburgh) made its early wealth from the Otago goldrush of the mid-19th century, although Maori occupation of the site goes back much further. Now it's an architecturally rich city with a youthful air – about a quarter of its population are under the age of 25. It's the starting point for a number of marine wildlife excursions, and for the SSR.

The designated route leaves Dunedin heading southwest and once you cross the Clutha River at Balclutha you enter the Catlins, a sparely populated and beautiful region that includes New Zealand's most southerly tip, Slope Point. There is so much to see along this coast, including many species of seal, penguin and dolphin. The Nuggets are rocky islets just offshore, and jagged Nugget Point, just a five-minute walk from the car park, is crowned by an unusual and often photographed lighthouse.

In the Catlins the road also passes the broad sandy beach of Cannibal Bay, Jack's Blowhole and the beautiful Pūrākaunui Falls, a staircase waterfall close to the road. At Waipati Beach the towering Cathedral Caves are accessible for only a couple of hours around low tide – don't get caught.

The Catlins, and the first leg of the SSR, end at Invercargill, New Zealand's most southerly city. Scottish whalers and missionaries were the first European settlers here; many of the streets are named after Scottish rivers and it is said that you can still hear a Scottish burr in the local accent.

Beyond Invercargill the SSR continues along the coast before turning inland to follow the edge of Fiordland National Park. The fertile farming landscape eventually gives way to mountain scenery. At Riverton, Te Hikoi Southern Journey

LEFT: A reflection of the Earl Mountains on the Mirror Lake, taken from the Milford Road.

is a museum worth an hour or so of your time. It tells the story of both Maori and European struggles to survive at this edge of the world.

Halfway along Te Waewae Bay the road strikes off northwards, soon arriving in Tuatapere, a village first settled by a group of Hungarian pioneers. It used to be a railhead for the local timber

ABOVE: The open road between Milford Sound and Te Anau overlooking Lake Te Anau.

FAR LEFT: You can meet some very friendly Keas, the world's only alpine, burrow-digging parrot.

LEFT: Slope Point is the southernmost point in New Zealand.

ABOVE RIGHT: A field of Russell Lupins in the Eglinton Valley in Fiordland National Park.

industry and there's a good logging museum here. The Clifden limestone cave system nearby is accessible to the public, and to a population of glow worms who appreciate its windless, damp environment.

The SSR climbs slowly through the valley of the Waiau River now, great for walking and fishing. The river flows out of Lake Manapouri, a large expanse of water stretching deep into Fiordland. From its eastern shore you can take a boat trip to its western end – there are no roads – and then a bus over mountainous Wilmot Pass to Doubtful Sound, one of the longest of the fiords. It was so named in 1770 by Captain Cook who was unsure that it would make a good harbour.

Manapouri is big, but Lake Te Anau a little further on is bigger: it is 65 km long and the largest body of freshwater in Australasia by volume. Although it sits at an altitude of 210 metres

(689 ft), it is 417 metres (1,368) deep; so much of it is below sea level. The town of Te Anau is a good base from which to explore the area by water and by land, and a good place to stop after another day's driving. Sunsets are vivid over the mountains beyond the lake, and another glow worm colony inhabits the Te Anau Caves, accessible by punt from the town.

Milford Sound, the most famous of South Island's fourteen saltwater fiords, lies at the end of a 119-km drive from here, following first the Eglinton River to its source and then descending with the Cleddau River and passing through the roughly dug Homer Tunnel to the magnificent fiord itself – towering sides framing a deep, 22-km-long inlet of Scandinavian beauty. The two permanent waterfalls which plummet into it are joined by hundreds of others during and after heavy rain: this is the wettest place in New Zealand. A cruise down Milford Sound,

consistently voted New Zealand's #1 tourist attraction, is a must either by day or overnight. Most vessels have underwater observatories.

Retracing your steps to Te Anau, the final leg of this trip takes you over high pastures to the shores of Lake Wakatipu, New Zealand's third largest lake, whose Z-shape is evidence of the powerful geological forces which have shaped and continue to shape this land. Journey's end is the alpine resort of Queenstown, a centre of outdoor activities all year round from river-rafting to snowboarding. You may prefer it for its spa facilities and gourmet food and wine produce. The road back to Dunedin is shorter and quicker than the road you got here by. You may not want to take it at all.

TOP: The Purakaunui Falls in The Catlins.

ABOVE: Wind-contorted pine trees battered into shape above Slope Point.

RIGHT: A time-lapse photo of Nugget Point Lighthouse and beyond, the hull-loving Nuggets. Drivers on the SSR can detour to the lighthouse or opt for a 20-minute walk to Roaring Bay.

Stelvio Pass

Italy

Length: 46 km, 29 miles
Start: Prad/Prato
Finish: Bormio
Highlights: Gomagoi, Dreisprachespitze, Selvio Glacier, Spondalunga, Bormio

The Stelvio Pass is a route for superlatives. Thanks to a 'fairground-ride' sequence of hairpin bends it achieves an astonishing vertical climb between Prad and the summit. Despite that, or perhaps because of it, it's as popular with cyclists as it is with motorists.

On one day every year in late August or early September, the Italian authorities close the Stelvio Pass to everyone except cyclists. Every year around 12,000 cyclists accept the gift of a clear road and put their leg muscles through this most gruelling of courses; and every year thousands of motorists wonder why the cyclists don't just drive over it and save themselves the pain. The answer is, of course, as Everest mountaineer George Mallory explained, because it's there.

It's been there since it was completed in 1825. It was a vital link in the transport network of the Austrian Empire of the time, connecting the

province of Tyrol with Lombardy (which Austria had reclaimed following the fall of Napoleon). In due course Lombardy seceded from Austria to join the newly formed country of Italy, and for a time Stelvio Pass marked the border between Italy and Austria.

When the Austrian Empire was dismantled at the end of the First World War, Tyrol was divided in two; North Tyrol remained in Austria but South Tyrol was reassigned to Italy. This is why on the Tyrolean side of the Pass most still speak a form of German and why many places have two names. For example the pass is known as both Passo dello Stelvio (Italian) and Stilfserjoch (Tyrolean).

Prad (or Prato), the town from which the Stelvio road leaves, is 97 per cent German-speaking. It's a small farming community in a wide, flat valley surrounded by high peaks. As you leave it heading southwest on route SS38 you can already see the summit of your ride in the distance; but soon the walls of the valley crowd in and there is barely room for the road and the

RIGHT: The long and winding road that leads to the Stelvio Pass. Alfa Romeo have named their speedy SUV after it.

tumbling mountain river which hurtles past you on its way back to Prad.

At Stilfsbrücke (Ponte di Stelvio, Stelvio Bridge) the route crosses the river and continues to Gomagoi, whose houses are pressed against the hillside to allow the road to pass through. Here there are well-preserved remains of defensive bunkers built by the Austrian Army during the Great War. Beyond Gomagoi there are again glimpses of the top of the pass and soon, in rapid succession, the first two of some 70 hairpin bends on this route.

There are two more at the small skiing village of Trafoi, and now the road is really gaining height, rising through forest high above the valley floor. Two more past Trafoi, then suddenly – whoa! – they start to come in scribbled masses. A sequence of ten at once, then eighteen, then another fourteen above the tree line: between the alpine pastures of Trafoi and the summit of Stelvio, a distance of just 13 km, there are 44 tight hairpins, stacked above each other like rungs on a ladder. The only way out of this is up and over.

At the Pass itself there is a cluster of hotels, restaurants and souvenir bazaars and a very modern church, where you can give thanks for your arrival and safe avoidance of cyclists on the way up. A cable car takes you to the top of the Stelvio Glacier; it's usually a year-round ski area, although in 2017 a heatwave forced its closure for the first time in 90 years.

You will certainly want to get out and stretch your legs. Unless you are a weary cyclist, you should take the short steep walk north to the summit of the Dreisprachespitze, 'Three Languages Peak'. Technically it is just over the border in Switzerland, and its location is where German, Italian and the Swiss language of Romansh all meet. The views from it are spectacular in any language.

Now all you have to do is get down from here. At first the road onwards to Bormio falls steadily away in this high mountain wilderness until suddenly at Spondalunga the valley opens up beneath you and you are forced into another dizzying descent on 14 hairpin bends.

Snow sheds and tunnels protect you from the worst of the mountain to which the road now clings, and a few more twists and turns lower you back below the tree line. Now the valley begins to open out, and before you know it you are on the outskirts of Bormio, an ancient settlement. Its hot springs, still in use today, were known to the Romans. You pass the old health resort of Bormio Spa, worth a stop for its pretty chapel of St Martin. The new and more glamorous Spa Hotel is further down the valley.

Bormio's medieval centre reflects its position on the trade route from Venice to Switzerland. Now it is an important skiing destination, and its Stelvio piste, named after the pass, is one of the toughest on the championship circuit.

The Stelvio road ends here, exhausted after threading its way back and forth across hills and mountains for the past 46 km. The road's iconic status has convinced both motorcycle manufacturer Moto Guzzi and sports car legend Alfa Romeo to name models after it.

TOP LEFT: The church of St Maria at Trafoi in the Stelvio Valley.

OPPOSITE: Like many Alpine passes, the Passio dello Stelvio is only open between May and November.

ABOVE: At 2,760 metres (9,055 ft), it is the highest finish on any of cycling's three Grand Tours. *Top Gear* voted it the most exhilarating driving road in the world.

RIGHT: After Italian cyclist Fausto Coppi won a classic stage of the Giro d'Italia up the climb to the Stelvio Pass it is forever linked with his name.

The Strip: Las Vegas

Nevada, USA

Length: 4.2 miles, 6.8 km
Start: 'Welcome to Fabulous Las Vegas' sign
Finish: Neon Museum
Highlights: The Luxor, The Bellagio, Caesar's Palace, The Mirage, Circus Circus

Drive 'The Strip' at night and the neon will blow you away. With good reason Las Vegas has been called the Jewel of the Desert. Like moths to a flame, 35 million visitors per year are drawn to the lights of this infamous playground. It's worth hiring something extravagant for this one, perhaps a Mustang, a Chevy or a Corvette.

Steve Wynn, Las Vegas hotel tycoon, has said, 'Las Vegas is sort of like how God would do it if he had money.' This must be one of the few drives that is more spectacular at night than during the day and while Las Vegas is famous for its gambling and culture of no-holds excess, it is also a city of incredible architectural fantasy lands and homages to our global heritage.

Start at the iconic 'Welcome to Fabulous Las Vegas' sign and head north on Las Vegas Boulevard. The first building you pass on your right, the Little Church of the West, is also the oldest building on the strip and made famous by Elvis in *Viva Las Vegas* – stop here for your Presley-style impromptu wedding!

The first of the big hotels, the Mandalay Bay, greets you on your left and just past it looms the enormous pyramid of the Luxor, containing the largest atrium in the world and topped with the Sky Beam, slicing into the sky from its pinnacle. This 42.3 billion-candela ray of light is the strongest beam in the world – you can't miss it. Sitting at the front entrance is a replica of the Great Sphinx of Giza, even larger than the original.

Next, on your left is the Disneyesque castle of Excalibur, shortly followed by New York-New York. No need to travel across the country to see the Empire State Building, the Chrysler Building, the Statue of Liberty, the Soldiers and Sailors Monument, the Whitney Museum of American Art, the Main Immigration Building of Ellis Island, or Grand Central Terminal; they're all here!

On your right you see the MGM Grand, followed by M&Ms World, the Coca Cola store, the Hard Rock Café, and other famously American brands all lit up in bright neon. As a contrast, to the left you won't miss the acres of glass of what claims to be the most technologically advanced hotel ever built, the Aria, fronted by the neon glow of brands epitomizing wealth and luxury – Gucci, Dolce & Gabana, YSL, Louis Vuitton, Prada.

Slightly further down the strip you arrive in Paris, with a half-scale replica of the Eiffel Tower, a two-thirds size

LEFT: Looking south past the Luxor pyramid, with The Strip and the Mandalay Bay resort hotel on the left.

OPPOSITE: The iconic Western Neon sign designed by Betty Willis in 1959 and one of the few things to remain unchanged.

Arc de Triomphe, and a replica of La Fontaine des Mers. Opposite is the Bellagio, famous for its high stakes poker. Evoking the sense of a big poker win are the Fountains of Bellagio, a choreographed water feature and light show occupying eight acres (every 15 minutes from 8pm until midnight). Next door is the Roman splendour of Caesar's Palace, famous throughout its history for hosting performances from the very greatest entertainers, from Frank Sinatra, Sammy Davis Jr. and Dean Martin through to Cher, Diana Ross, Celine Dion and Elton John.

Further down the strip stands the spectacle of the Mirage: drive by at 8, 9 or 10pm to see the volcano erupt. This is followed by Treasure Island, with its palm-clad cliffs and pirate ships; the Italian splendour of the Palazzo; and the Venetian, the second largest hotel in the world. You don't need to travel all the way to Venice for a gondola ride.

Passing the luxury of The Wynn, considered one of the top hotels in the world, the strip becomes more subdued as you head towards downtown Las Vegas. You pass Circus Circus on your left, the largest permanent big top in the world; but from here Las Vegas Boulevard slowly transforms itself into an almost normal American town, albeit with a few more motels, slots and the towering Stratosphere Tower. Keep on driving through downtown to the Neon Museum which tells the history of Sin City's taste for showy excess – although this is one of the few daytime-only stops on this tour.

Finally, turn round and do it all again, and remember: what happens in Vegas stays in Vegas!

ABOVE LEFT: Looking east across The Strip with the battlements of Excalibur in the foregound, New York-New York to the left, and across The Strip, the MGM, illuminated in green.

LEFT: New York-New York – so good they built it twice.

TOP: The busy junction where East Flamigo Road crosses The Strip with the Paris resort hotel beyond.

MIDDLE: Opened in 2014, the 168-metre (550-ft) High Roller observation wheel is attached to The LINQ.

ABOVE: The north end of The Strip as it passes right below the Stratosphere Tower.

RIGHT: The fauxest of the faux, the Venetian, complete with motorized gondolas, occupies the site of the old Sands Hotel.

The Stuart Highway

Northern Territories, Australia

Length: 1,496 km, 930 miles
Start: Darwin
Finish: Alice Springs
Highlights: Adelaide River, Daly Waters, Tennant Creek, Alice Springs

On the Stuart Highway, it is said, you are more likely to run over a kangaroo than see another human being. If you're the sort of driver who likes to be alone with their thoughts while behind the wheel, then this is the 1,500-km road trip for you.

One thing to think about as you drive the Stuart Highway is the man in whose footsteps you are following. In 1861–62 John McDouall Stuart led the first expedition successfully to cross the continent of Australia from south to north and back again – on foot. It was his sixth attempt and built on the crucial discoveries of water holes made on his earlier outings. For his persistence and eventual success he is rightly honoured as one of the greatest from the Golden Age of the Explorer.

This journey starts, appropriately, beside a statue of Stuart in Darwin in the Northern Territories at the junction of Smith and Knuckey. Here an effigy of the bearded wanderer points to the north coast of Australia which he had at last reached, nine months after leaving the south coast at Port Augusta. From here, leave town on Highway 1.

Near the Darwin suburb of Humpty Doo you can join a cruise on the Adelaide River. From the decks, cruise staff feed saltwater crocodiles, which leap bodily out of the water to take the offered food. The snap of their jaws is a loud reminder that you really don't want to go swimming around here.

The small town of Adelaide River 80 km further south is typical of many settlements along the Stuart Highway. Originally built for constructors of the telegraph line from Darwin to Adelaide in 1872, it grew when gold was discovered in the area. The railroad arrived in 1888 and today there's a museum with rolling stock from the original North Australia Railway Company, which ceased regular services in 1976. Water buffalo hunters used the railway to export the hides; and also on show, in the local inn, is the preserved body of Charlie the Buffalo, one of the stars of the film *Crocodile Dundee*.

LEFT: Termite mounds are a regular sight off the Stuart Highway.

character, and a very direct connection with John McDouall Stuart. Still growing here is the tree into which Stuart carved the initial S when he found freshwater springs here on one of his earlier expeditions.

TOP: The Stuart Highway is the natural habitat for mighty road trains, which take a lot of stopping.

ABOVE: A group of feral camels grazing just off the Stuart Highway in the Northern Territory.

ABOVE RIGHT: The remains of an expansive salt works on Lake Hart near Woomera.

OPPOSITE: Take a short detour off the Stuart Highway at the village of Daly Waters to stop for fuel, but more importantly visit the historic pub (not shown), an outback legend.

Trees and bushes are still dense beside the road here. The further south you get, the patchier the ground cover becomes and the red desert soil starts to show through. Wildlife depends on the vegetation and there's plenty of roadkill on the Highway, often attended by a scavenging wedge-tailed eagle. Don't assume that it will fly away out of your path – this large bird needs a bit of time to get airborne.

Daly Waters, 590 km south of Darwin, has a historic airfield, an outback pub of enormous

Many 'towns' along the Stuart Highway are little more than a petrol pump and a rest room. However, Tennant Creek, 500 km north of Alice Springs and just south of the meeting of the Stuart and Barkly Highways, has a substantial population of around 3,000 and plenty of amenities for the weary traveller. This is prime cattle-grazing country, the basis for the town's wealth along with the mining of minerals in the area. Gold was discovered just north of Tennant Creek in the 1920s, prompting Australia's last goldrush to date.

Fully half the town's population is Aboriginal and south of Tennant Creek lies one of the must-sees of the Stuart Highway, the Devil's Marbles – or to give them their correct name, Karlu Karlu. These huge rounded boulders, broken from granite outcrops and weathered by water, have a place in several traditional Aboriginal Dreamings and are among the oldest religious sites in the world. Visit them with respect.

Periodically on your journey you will have seen the tracks of the celebrated Ghan Railway. Although it doesn't follow the Stuart Highway completely, it too connects Darwin and Adelaide. The Ghan gets its name from the Afghans originally hired to drive the camels which were used in expeditions into the Australian interior. The line south of Adelaide was built in 1929, but before 2004 the journey north of Alice Springs could only be made by driving the Stuart Highway.

At that time the road was an unmade track, vulnerable to rain and interrupted by creeks along the way. Only with the advent of war and the need to supply Australian defence forces in the north was the paving of the road begun in 1940. That work was only completed in the 1980s.

Just before your entry into Alice Springs you cross the Tropic of Capricorn. Beyond Alice Springs, road and rail continue south to the coast. But Alice, known as Stuart until 1933, is our destination for now. Alice is the home of the Flying Doctor Service, the Camel Cup and the Henley-on-Todd Regatta in which boats race on the dry bed of the Todd River. Alice Todd was the wife of a former Postmaster General of South Australia on whose watch the Springs were discovered.

One final word of warning: if you see a cloud of dust approaching, get out of the way. It may be a road-train, a truck towing three or more trailers in a row. Once these heavy freight loads get up to speed on the open road of the Stuart Highway, they don't like to slow down. For anything. Where do you think all that roadkill comes from?

Targa Florio

Sicily, Italy

Length: 72 km, 45 miles
Start/Finish: Cerda
Highlights: Caltavuturo, Collesano, Cerda

The Targa Florio was a legendary sports car race run on public roads around the island of Sicily. It ran for over 70 years before concerns about safety forced its closure in 1977.

You can still follow the last iteration of the route today. The Targa Florio was the brainchild of Vincenzo Florio, a member of a wealthy Sicilian family with interests in wine, shipping and newspapers. His passion was the new sport of motor-racing and as a driver he won the Targa Rignano, named after an Italian count of that

RIGHT: Before he left the Red Bull team, F1 driver Daniel Ricciardo drove the Alfa Romeo T33 that his mentor Helmut Marko drove in the 1972 Targa Florio.

BELOW: A sign outside Cerda shows the three different routes that can be taken.

name. He decided in 1906 that he would create a race bearing his own family name. Targa means plaque, and Florio commissioned the leading artists of the day to design the prize for the race. He also launched a motoring magazine to promote it. The spirit of the age was Speed, and he wanted his race to embody it. 'I created it,' he said, 'to challenge time.'

From 1951 the race was run on 11 laps of a circuit in the Madonie mountains in the north of Sicily, the Circuito Piccolo delle Madonie. Piccolo – small – it may have been; but it was certainly not short on difficulty. In its 72 km it has more than 700 corners, an average of more than ten per kilometre. No one has reached an average speed of more than 130kph (80mph) and you shouldn't try.

From Cerda, where you can still see signs of the old starting line, you follow the route in an anticlockwise direction, heading south on route SS120. Soon the road starts to hairpin back and forth on its way up to Caltavuturo, the Fort of the Vultures, on a plateau beneath the forbidding mountain Rocca di Sciara. It's a town of narrow streets with a fine castle and a bloody role in the history of land rights. This is the most southerly, and the highest point on the Targa. From here it turns north-eastwards on the SP24 and the SP9 to Collesano, a fascinating hilltown with a Greek, Arab and Norman past and the official Targa Florio Museum.

From Collesano the road plunges down to the sea at Campofelice de Roccella where it enjoys the race route's only straight section on 6.6 km of SS13. It can't last, and soon the road turns south again on the SS120 to return to Cerda, where there is a museum dedicated to the race's founder.

Although Alfa Romeo, Ferrari, Lancia, and Maserati all flew the Italian flag with success at the Targa Florio, Porsche owned the race with a record of eleven wins. It is for this race that the

911 Targa is named. The fastest ever lap was posted by Finnish driver Leo Kinnunen in 1970 in a Porsche 908/3: 33 minutes and 36 seconds. If you get to drive the Targa in a Porsche, or any other classic sports car – then, lucky you.

RIGHT: Daniel Ricciardo eases the Alfa Romeo T33 through a hairpin on his promotional run for Red Bull.

BELOW: Double dented roadside barriers bear witness to the temptation for drivers to set a time on the route.

OPPOSITE: Having completed the classic 72-km circuit, why not explore Sicily further with the 148-km Circuito Grande.

OPPOSITE BOTTOM: Two photos of the start/finish and pits area in Cerda, which are still preserved. There has been a resurgence of classic car runs on the Targa Florio in recent years taking on the counter-clockwise Circuito Piccolo.

Transfagarasan Road

Romania

Length: 114 km, 71 miles
Start: Cârțișoara, Transylvania
Finish: Pitești, Walachia
Highlights: Lake Bâlea and the Bâlea Waterfall, Poienari Castle

Few people have cause to remember Nicolae Ceaușescu with any fondness, but the Romanian dictator did manage to order the construction of the Transfăgărășan Road.

Fearing an event similar to the 1968 Soviet invasion of Czechoslovakia, Ceaușescu needed an efficient way of transporting troops over the Făgăraș Mountains, part of the southern Carpathians. Starting in 1970, his soldiers took four and a half years and used six million kilos of dynamite to blast the 114-km Route 7 between Cârțișoara in Transylvania and Pitești in Walachia.

Since then, Route 7, also known as DN 7C, has been superseded by faster roads that have the added benefit of remaining open for the six or seven months a year when the Transfăgărășan Road is shut by snow. However, what it lacks in modern comforts and accessability, the road makes up for in wild vistas and enjoyably demanding driving.

The start point is 487 metres (1,598 ft) above sea level. Its highest point, by Lake Bâlea, is at 2,042 metres (6,700 ft). While the route involves lots of ascent and descent, it was designed for heavy military vehicles to grind up and down. Long S-curves and switchbacks are the norm rather than steep gradients. The average speed, when not in a tank, is 40kph. Five tunnels, 27 viaducts and 831 small bridges add interest.

Once past the glacial Lake Bâlea, the route passes through the longest road tunnel in Romania. The 887-metre-long tunnel marks a distinct change in scenery. To the north, the landscape is harsh and mountainous. Snow in August is not unheard of. South of the tunnel, the road begins to gently descend into verdant valleys.

Many visitors choose to stretch their legs with a stop to admire the Bâlea Waterfall which is located to the north of the tunnel. Others break their journey on the southern side of the tunnel and take a stroll around the Vidraru Lake and dam, an artificial lake created in 1965 to provide hydroelectricity.

Arguably the most popular detour on the Transfăgărășan Road is a stop to climb the 1,450 steps to the ruins of Poenari Castle. Perched on a cliff over the Argeș River, the fortress was a firm favourite with a certain Dracula. The inspiration for Bram Stoker's vampire was also known as Vlad the Impaler. Possibly the only Romanian to have a reputation worse than that of Ceaușescu.

BELOW: Bâlea Lake, a glacial lake situated at 2,034 metres (6,673 ft), is close to the highest point of the route.

Trolls' Path

Norway

Length: 55 km, 34 miles
Start: Åndalsnes
Finish: Valldallen
Highlights: Stigfossen waterfall, Trolls' Ladder hairpin bends, Trollstigen Visitor Centre, Kongen and Dronninga mountains

According to Norse mythology, some species of trolls roam the countryside at night but turn into mountains as the sun rises. Perhaps it's best to stick to daylight hours when driving Norway's worryingly narrow Trolls' Path.

The Trolls' Path or Trollstigen, is a dramatic section of Norwegian County Road 63. Located in the north-west of the country, Road 63 snakes from Åndalsnes on Romsdalsfjorden south to Valldallen on the Storfjorden. From there, motorists can choose to take the ferry from Linge Pier across the fjord to Eidsdal and then continue to the head of the Geirangerfjord; a location on UNESCO's World Heritage List since 2005. The Trollstigen section, also known as the Trolls' Ladder, was built over the traces of a

centuries-old pack road mountain pass which linked the then villages of Åndalsnes and Valldall. The new road was opened by King Haakon VII in July 1936. In 2012, the road was improved and designated a national tourist route. It is very much a seasonal attraction: snow and ice ensure that the road, with a 9 per cent incline and potential rock falls, is usually closed from October to May.

The long winter season meant that the road took eight years to construct. Each of the eleven hairpin bends was either hand-carved from the rock or built by stone laid on top of the base rock. Most of the bends are named after the foremen that supervised their construction.

There are several viewpoints along the Trollstigen route. For many, the road bridge across the Stigfossen waterfall is a highlight. Others enjoy the sweeping vistas provided by

LEFT: The snaking mountain approach road is the most famous in Norway.

the angular Trollstigen Visitor Centre, a striking building designed to blend into the landscape by Reiulf Ramstad Architects. As well as a cafe and museum detailing the history of the road, this development has a number of look-out points including one steel and glass construction which juts out from a ledge 200 metres (656 ft) above the twisting road.

The Trollstigen Centre is on a plateau which is 853 metres (2,799 ft) above sea level. The eleven hairpin bends and steep incline mean that drivers will feel every one of those metres. However, the platform is dwarfed by surrounding mountains. These include Kongen, the king, and Dronninga, the queen. The former reaches 1,614 metres (5,295 ft) into the sky. The trolls are obviously quite tall in Norway.

TOP: Learner drivers in Norway do not have to learn this warning sign as part of the Norwegian Highway Code.

LEFT AND RIGHT: At the top of the Trolls' Ladder, there is a viewing platform, Trollstigheim, which gives an impressive view of the Stigfossen waterfall (also pictured right) as it thunders beneath the overhang.

Val d'Orcia

Italy

The Val d'Orcia lies to the south of the fine medieval city of Siena. A circular tour around this gentle Tuscan countryside takes you over rolling hills and through dusty, ancient villages and towns. Its landscape has inspired artists and photographers for centuries.

Length: 140 km, 87 miles
Start/Finish: Siena
Highlights: Montalcino, San Quirico d'Orcia, Pienza, Capella della Madonna di Vitaleta, Montepulciano

Siena will need no introduction to lovers of Italy. Famous for the Palio, a horse race through city streets by teams from competing districts of the old town, Siena is blessed with magnificent 12th- and 13th-century architecture and artworks by masters of the period. The graceful cathedral and the buildings around the Piazza del Campo are religious and secular statements of wealth and power.

Siena's riches came in part from the lands through which this road trip passes. Leaving the city southbound on the SR2, you keep the small stream of the Torrente Arbia on your left as you follow it downstream. The road crosses it finally at Ponte Arbia, one of many small villages along the way built of red brick and yellowing stucco. Buonconvento a few kilometres ahead is a small settlement – it's name means 'blessed place' – which was fortified by Siena. You can still see traces of the walls and a handsome clock tower in the old centre.

About a kilometre south of here turn right onto the SP45, climbing through olive groves and vinyeards towards Montalcino. This is a classic Sienese hill town, all narrow streets and well endowed churches. It held out for four years after Siena itself succumbed to the Medici dynasty of Florence, and when you see Montalcino's fortress you'll understand how. Today its fortunes rest on the popularity of its local wine, Brunello de Montalcino. From its commanding heights the views in every direction are superb.

Leave Montalcino on the SP14 towards San Qurico d'Orcia. At the point where you rejoin the SR2 you may be lucky enough to see a steam-hauled vintage train. The service between Monte Antico to the south and Asciano at the centre of this circular drive was withdrawn in 1994, but the line reopened as a heritage railway only two years later. San Quirico lies on the traditional pilgrim route of St Francis's Way, leading to Assisi in the east. St Francis is the patron saint of animals and in San Quirico you'll see carvings of lions, crocodiles and more fearsome monsters in the town's Romanesque Collegiate Church.

Between San Quirico and Pienza along the SP146 you'll pass the tiny, pretty Chapel of the Madonna of Vitaleta, all alone in the middle of a field. It's the subject of a hundred postcards and a classic image of Tuscany. It used to hold

RIGHT: An early summer-morning view across the Val d'Orcia.

a sculpture of the Virgin Mary by the brilliant ceramicist Andrea della Robbia which is now in the church of the same name back in San Quirico.

Pienza stands high on a hill, queen of all it surveys. Its central piazza is a gem of renaissance architecture, surrounded by the town hall, two palaces and the cathedral. The finest of them is Palazzo Piccolomini. Silvo Piccolomini became Pope Pius II and decided to transform his home village of Pienza into a planned town following the aesthetic ideals of the Italian Rennaissance. Construction began in 1459, a year after his

ABOVE: The beautiful hilltop village of Pienza.

LEFT: Early morning at the celebrated pool in the thermal spa village of Bagno Vignoni.

elevation to the papacy. The beautiful garden within his palace sits on top of stables for a hundred horses.

Continue east from Pienza on the SP146 to Montepulciano, stopping just before you enter the walled town to visit the church of San Biagio. It's a gleaming white 16th-century building set in fields on the terraces to the west of the town. There's something about its dignified neoclassical beauty which demands your inner peace; but also, you should try clapping or singing inside it to test its famous acoustics.

Montepulciano is famed for its food and drink, especially its Vino Nobile di Montepulciano. Although today it is in the province of Siena, it historically resisted Siena's military advances, siding instead with Florence. The town walls are above you as you approach Montepulciano from San Biagio, and its castle is the Fortezza Medicea, named after the powerful Florentine family. The medieval centre is largely traffic-free and a delight to walk around.

From Montepulciano your way back to Siena is via two more fine hill towns, Sinalunga and Asciano, the latter with town walls paid for by Siena in 1351. Asciano is the northern terminus of the Val d'Orcia heritage railway. Just to the south of it is the Benedictine monastery of Monte Oliveto Maggiore, a large complex of ecclesiastical buildings particularly famous for the frescoes in its cloisters.

Some come to Tuscany for the scenery, others for the remarkable wealth of art and architecture. Most of the towns on this road trip began life as Etruscan settlements in the first millennium BC and this is a region with a long, sophisticated cultural history. It has been fought for and farmed for at least 3000 years, and the results are all around you. Stop, and admire the view.

ABOVE LEFT: Pecora sheep whose milk is used to make local Pecorino cheese in Vergelle, near Montalcino.

TOP: One of the most photographed chapels in Tuscany, the Capella di Vitaleta at sunrise. It was formerly the home of a famous Renaissance sculpture of the Madonna, since moved to San Quirico.

ABOVE: A view from the grand Pulcinella Tower looking down into the main square at Montepulciano.

The White Mountain Ring

New Hampshire, USA

Length: 100 miles, 160 km
Start/Finish: North Woodstock
Highlights: Flume Gorge, Cannon Mountain, Mount Washington Cog Railway, Silver Cascade, Conway Scenic Railroad, Albany Covered Bridge, Lost River Gorge

Magnificent views abound in the White Mountains, winter, spring, summer or fall. But it's the fall colours that this epic part of New England is most famous for.

The White Mountains in New Hampshire – one of the six New England states – are a popular holiday destination because they lie within striking distance of Boston, New York and Montreal, and because they offer a rich mix of history, outdoor activity and magnificent scenery. The White Mountain Ring is a comfortable day's driving with stops for highlights along the way. This particular route takes you around and through the range and crosses it on routes which have been used as trails for centuries. It doesn't matter in which direction you tackle this circular outing, or where you start and finish.

We'll go clockwise, starting in the New Hampshire village of North Woodstock, where there is a useful White Mountains Visitor Center. Heading north from here on Route 3 the road

climbs through Franconia Notch, squeezing between Mount Lafayette and Cannon Mountain. On the way to the summit, stop at Flume Gorge, which you can descend into on a wooden walkway below Avalanche Falls.

You can ascend Cannon Mountain the easy way by the Cannon Mountain Aerial Tramway. Its imposing cliffs once included The Old Man of the Mountains, a natural rock formation with the profile of a human face. Much beloved of Hampshirites, the Old Man sat above beautiful Profile Lake, and was adopted as the state emblem in 1945. Frost and ice took their toll and it collapsed in 2003, greatly mourned.

As Route 3 veers westwards along the shores of Echo Lake, it bypasses the charming New England villages of Franconia, Bethlehem and Littleton, each with their own mountain setting. A detour from Route 3 at Twin Mountain takes you to the most magical of them all, Santa's Village, whose shows and rides are open all year round.

ABOVE RIGHT: Flume Gorge in the Franconia Notch State Park.

RIGHT: A covered bridge over the Pemigewasset River, known locally as 'The Pemi', in Franconia Notch State Park.

OPPOSITE: Fall colour at Echo Lake at the northern end of Franconia Notch: the 'notch' being the mountain pass.

The main route continues now on Route 302, following the Ammonoosac River eastwards and upstream. A trail of about a mile along the riverbank gets you up close to the tumbling Lower Ammonoosac Falls. The Ammonoosac rises on the western slopes of Mount Washington, the highest peak in the north-eastern states at 1,917 metres (6,288 ft). Near the village of Fabyan, a cog railway built in 1869 takes you up through forests to the top of Mount Washington, but beware: for most of the 20th century Washington held the record for the strongest wind ever recorded on our planet, 372kph (231mph).

Mount Washington lies in the Presidential Range, a ridge of peaks named after American leaders including Mount Adams, Mount Jefferson, Mount Madison and so on. President Eisenhower is the most recent honoree – New Hampshire's attempt to rename one summit Mount Reagan has not so far been recognized by the US Government.

As the road veers south it passes through Crawford Notch, another pass of remarkable natural beauty. Watch out for Elephant Head, a rocky outcrop that, as the name suggests, looks from a certain angle like the front end of a pachyderm. A little further on, the road passes

through Attitash at Roger's Crossing, one of many White Mountain ski resorts. Attitash caters for summer visitors too with zipwires and a mountain rollercoaster. At Glen village there's a popular family attraction, Story Land.

Turning south once more the route brings you to Conway, a large tourist centre. One of Conway's highlights is the Conway Scenic Railroad, with its beautifully restored 19th-century station buildings. Preserved steam and diesel engines run from here through Crawford Notch to Fabyan in evocative old railroad carriages, giving you a different perspective on the landscape.

At Conway the White Mountain Ring leaves Route 302 and the Saco River which it has been following since Fabyan. It now turns for home along Route 112, also known as the Kancamagus Highway. This is the final, glorious section of the route, 35 miles climbing with the Swift River, a tributary of the Saco, to near its source on the flanks of Mount Kancamagus. Along the way there are waterfalls aplenty, including the Lower Falls next to Albany Covered Bridge and the aptly named Rocky Gorge.

After the grand views of the White Mountains from the highest point on the road, it descends to Lincoln and back to North Woodstock. Your 100 miles are up. If you want more, then nearby in the pass of Kinsman Notch is the Lost River Gorge, filled with the giant boulders of a collapsed cave, from which you can walk or crawl into other caves in the system.

ABOVE LEFT: The vintage Mount Washington Cog Railway trains carry tourists to the summit near Bretton Woods.

TOP: A less inclined train pulls into the Victorian Conway Station, home to the Conway Scenic Railroad.

ABOVE: The Sunny Day Diner in Lincoln, New Hampshire; open in all weathers.

LEFT: A 19th-century covered bridge over the Swift River at Albany, New Hampshire.

between two pretty waterfalls just a short walk away, the Flume and Silver Cascades.

Before the establishment of the White Mountain National Forest the area was a centre of the logging industry, and today you can see many traces of it – for example, the abandoned ghost town of Livermore near Hart's Location on Route 302. As the road turns back eastwards it passes

The White Mountain Ring is a beautiful route. There are plenty of man-made attractions to enjoy all the way round, but the real star of the show is Mother Nature herself; the rugged landscape and the passes first opened up by Native Americans like Kancamagus (for whom the highway is named) and later travelled by the first pioneering Europeans.

The Wild Atlantic Way

Ireland

Length: 2,500 km, 1,600 miles
Start: Kinsale, Co Cork
Finish: Inishowen Peninsula, Ulster
Highlights: Ring of Kerry, Dingle, Cliffs of Moher, Aran Islands, Connemara, Westport, Ballyshannon, Fanad Peninsula

The Wild Atlantic Way celebrates the rugged extremities of Ireland's Atlantic-carved west coast, a landscape as dramatic as any in Europe.

Chiselled and battered by the fierce storms and seas of the Atlantic Ocean, Ireland looks towards America from a coast of windswept flats, towering cliffs and long-fingered peninsulas.

The Wild Atlantic Way was launched in 2014 to encourage people to explore the country which lies beyond the tourist traps of Dublin and Cork's famous Blarney Stone. At around 2,500 km it can be completed in a week, driving just a few hours

a day and stopping for occasional highlights. But there are so many natural and man-made wonders along the way that you might want to take two weeks over it.

In Ireland they drive on the left, so the best advice is to travel the Wild Atlantic Way from south to north. Not only will you be closer to the sea but it will be easier to pull over for stops and photographs. The route is well signed. Many

of the roads which make up the Way are slow, narrow and winding; don't expect to speed to your destination. Like a pint of Guinness, the Way is something to be savoured, not rushed.

The route starts in Kinsale, a little over three hours' drive from Dublin. Kinsale is a historic port with a rich military past. The geography of this south-western corner of the country consists of long sheltered estuaries warmed by the Gulf Stream, havens not only for sailors but for wild birds and, further out to sea, whales and dolphins.

Driving west through Clonakilty and Skibbereen you will find signs to Sheep's Head, where you will have your first sight of the open Atlantic Ocean and see the first of many lighthouses along the route. On a seven-day trip, the small town of Kenmare makes a good first night stop. It boasts one of the largest prehistoric stone circles in the area and plenty of more modern facilities for the hungry traveller.

Kenmare is good launching point for Day Two, which follows two long-established scenic drives

ABOVE: Storm waves lash against the cliffs of Belmullet, County Mayo.

RIGHT: The distinctive Benbulben Mountain in County Sligo overlooking the Wild Atlantic Way.

– the Ring of Kerry and the Dingle Peninsula. The Ring of Kerry (a circuit with its own 'crown' signage) can be extended to incorporate Valentia Island, accessible by roadbridge or ferry, where the first commercial transatlantic cable terminated and where dinosaurs once walked – you can see their fossilized footprints. Other highlights include the imposing Staigue Iron Age fort and Rossbeigh Beach. The roads are particularly narrow and the many coach trips which travel the Ring all do so in an anticlockwise direction to avoid having to pass each other.

The Dingle Peninsula is rich in prehistoric and medieval history. The pretty town of Dingle on its southern shore has been a busy fishing port since the 12th century. At the western end of the peninsula you can see what remains of the ship MV Ranga, wrecked on the rocks of Dunmore Head in 1982. Its broken, rusting bow is a reminder of the force of the Atlantic which has shaped this shore.

Beyond Tralee – where they filmed majestic beach scenes in *Ryan's Daughter* – and Listowel

the Atlantic Ocean meets the estuary of the mighty Shannon river, Ireland's longest, which drains a full fifth of all the country's landmass. It's the boundary between County Limerick and County Clare and a good place to end a day's driving. The first bridge across it is in Limerick town, but the ferry from Tarbert to Killimer will save you over 210 km (130 miles).

County Clare's coast is one of Ireland's natural wonders. Starting with the lighthouse at Loop Head, the landscape and the road drop down to

run along the shore at Spanish Point – a reminder of the scattered vessels of the Spanish Armada which passed this way in 1588, limping back to Spain. The road climbs gradually to Hag's Head, the southern end of the sheer, fortress-like Cliffs of Moher. For 18 km the cliffs form an unbroken barrier between sea and land, rising to a height of 214 metres (702 ft).

The vibrant university town of Galway makes a fitting stopover after the exhilaration of the clifftop drive. Join the evening promenade, enjoy fine seafood and above all, go to a pub for an informal session of traditional Irish music.

North and west of Galway you enter what Oscar Wilde called the 'strange beauty' of Connemara. If you have time, a trip to the Aran Islands is unforgettable. They lie out in the Atlantic, about an hour by boat (or ten minutes by air) off the Connemara coast and seemingly untouched by

the 21st or even the 20th century – although one of them became the fictional Craggy Island for the comedy series *Father Ted*.

Connemara itself is a sparsely populated mosaic of lakes and mountains, roamed by wild Connemara ponies, descendants of horses that swam ashore from shipwrecks of the Spanish Armada. Beyond the coastal villages of Clifden and Letterfrack, the Atlantic Way comes up against Killary Harbour, a long narrow natural stretch of seawater known as Ireland's only fjord and ground out thousands of years ago by a glacier.

After Killary the landscape softens and the route curves around the wide expanse of Clew Bay, studded with hundreds of tiny islets including Clare Island, once the home of Grainne O'Malley, queen of the pirates. At the head of the bay sits Westport. The town was built, like Edinburgh's

OPPOSITE: Running for 14 kilometres, the rigidly vertical Cliffs of Moher in County Clare rise 120 metres (390 ft) above the sea at Hag's Head, and reach their maximum height of 214 metres (702 ft) north of O'Brien's Tower.

ABOVE LEFT: You'll find a few of these on your journey; O'Neill's Bar and The Lighthouse Bar next door to each other in the village of Allihies, Cork.

ABOVE: It's a well-signposted route with its own Wild Atlantic Way graphic.

New Town, to a rigid Georgian street plan after the local landowner demolished a village to make space for his garden. Now it hosts at least ten annual festivals – eleven if you count the Clare Island Film Festival. If none of them take your fancy, the sunset over Clew Bay is reason enough to stop here.

From Westport the route follows the coastal fringes of County Mayo, skirting the wild Ballycroy National Park in the Nephin Mountains. This is a unique wildlife habitat of some 15,000 hectares of peatbog and the lakes and rivers that drain it. Along the way, Achill Island has the highest cliffs in Ireland. The Mullet Peninsula would be an island but for 400 metres of land in the village of Balmullet, once the scene of a stand-off between the government and workers who refused to build a fence across land occupied by leprechauns.

Continuing through Ballina which straddles the salmon fishing river of Moy, the Wild Atlantic Way arrives at Sligo town. The name means 'abundant in shells' and the plentiful supply of seafood has seen the area populated since the Stone Age. Many Neolithic structures remain. More recently the town has been home to cultural icons including author Bram Stoker. It is a centre for traditional music and more modern nightlife.

The road from Sligo to Donegal is short and fast, but there are plenty of distractions along the way. At Streedagh Point you can park on a long low sandbar built up by the relentless Atlantic tides, and explore this unique habitat. There are rich Neolithic remains at Creevykeel and around Ballyshannon, whose history also encompasses Viking raids and a medieval cemetery full of skeletons clutching pieces of quartz. A statue in the town honours blues guitarist Rory Gallagher who was born there.

North of Ballyshannon, Donegal Bay funnels waves onto the wide beach at Rossnowlagh,

attracting families and surfers. In the winter, rollers can reach 7 metres (30 ft) in height. Donegal Town faces the open ocean beyond the bay, with its back to the Blue Stack Mountains. Its name translates as 'fort of the foreigners' and its role as the seat of the ancient O'Connell dynasty places it at the heart of Irish history.

The final leg of the journey captures all the elements of the Wild Atlantic Way. There's Fintra beach at Killybegs; the cliffs of Slieve League leading to Rossan Point; and the exhilarating drive from there over Glengesh Pass to the village of Ardara. This north-western coast of Ireland, a popular choice for weekend homes, is as fragmented as any part of the Way, with hundreds of rocky inlets and tiny islands, especially around the area known as the Rosses north of Dunglow town. There's time for one last lighthouse on the extraordinary mixture of land and sea that is the Fanad peninsula.

At Rathmullan, in 1607, the flight of the Irish earls defeated by the English at the Battle of Kinsale marked the end of the old Gaelic order in Ireland. It's almost the end of your journey too – a ferry from Rathmullan across Lough Swilly takes you to Buncrana on the Inishowen peninsula. Buncrana is a lively tourist town and the last on the Wild Atlantic Way. From it you are only an hour's drive from Ireland's northernmost point, Malin Head. You can go no further.

LEFT: Doonagore Castle near the village of Doolin in County Clare. Built in the mid-16th century, a ship of the Spanish Armada was wrecked below the castle in September 1588. The Wild Atlantic Way is full of exhilarating views, littered with history and where a warm welcome for tourists is guaranteed.

Index

Credits

The large majority of the photos in this book were supplied by Alamy.com, with the exception of the following:

Frank Hopkinson/Pavilion Books: pages 8 top, 98, 99 top, 99 bottom right, 162, 163, 164, 165, 166, 167, 173, 174 bottom, 175 top, 190.

Getty Images: pages 12, 15 bottom left, 17, 63, 75, 77, 134, 135, 193 middle.

Jason Hawkes/Pavilion Books: 191, 192 top, 193 bottom.

Juliette Boulouis/Pavilion Books: page 97.

Karl Mondon/Pavilion Books: pages 192 bottom, 193 top, 193 right.

Porsche AG: page 200 bottom.

Red Bull: pages 199, 200 top.

Entries for Cotswold Loop, London Landmarks, Paris by Night, Route 66, written by Salamander Books editorial.

Thanks to Eliane Duchaussoie for Paris.